PRAYER

THE BELIEVER'S MASTER KEY

Pastor Nnaemeka C. Uchegbu

PRAYER
THE BELIEVER'S MASTER KEY

iUniverse books may be ordered through booksellers or by contacting:

iUniverse
1663 Liberty Drive
Bloomington, IN 47403
www.iuniverse.com
1-800-Authors (1-800-288-4677)

ISBN: 978-1-4917-3433-9 (sc)
ISBN: 978-1-4917-3501-5 (e)

Library of Congress Control Number: 2014908758

Print information available on the last page.

iUniverse rev. date: 03/06/2015

Contents

Foreword......vii

Introduction......ix

Epigraph xiii

1 What is Prayer?...... 1

2 Why Pray? 21

3 Types of Prayer......37

4 Conditions of Prayer. 67

5 Defects in prayer. 79

6 Dangers of Prayerlessness. 92

7 Benefits of Prayer. 97

Conclusion...... 111

Foreword

The discipline of prayer is a constant emphasis in the Scriptures. We are challenged to pray without ceasing and bring everything before the throne of grace in prayer.

Yet, this discipline remains one of the greatest weaknesses for believers. The priority of prayer and making time to invest in this important dimension of spiritual life has yet to grip the hearts of believers like it should.

In this volume, ***Prayer: The believer's Master Key***, Pastor Nnaemeka Uchegbu offers a very helpful and comprehensive overview of prayer as the spiritual discipline God always has intended. This is a very practical book…it gives great scriptural foundations for the discipline of prayer, honest teaching about what limits our prayer life, and a series of prayer points to actually put the principles into practice.

Pastor Nnaemeka has made a great contribution to the spiritual walk of all those reading these pages. May you enter into a new chapter in your prayer life…realizing that **prayer <u>is</u> the master key!**

Bishop Timothy A. Johnson
Minnesota Church Ministries Association

Introduction

Every Christian or believer in the word of God ought to be a living expression of Jesus Christ, the man of prayer, whose life was based on the fine art of divine communication. By several examples through-out his earthly ministry, Jesus of Nazareth proved in word and deed that prayer is an inevitable factor in the effective and meaningful relationship with God. Speaking with God was such an important function in Jesus' daily life that it became his trade-mark. Prayer was his master key, and he exploited every opportunity to pray to the fullest. It was the one thing he did before, during, and after all activities.

Jesus was so immersed in the attitude of prayer that one popular Sunday school worship-song, alluding to this secret of his success, summarized his life thus:

> ***"Prayer is the key, Prayer is the key,***
> ***Prayer is the master key.***

Jesus started with prayer,
And ended with prayer,
Prayer is the master key".

Indeed, prayer was Jesus secret door opener, the mystery of his victorious life and ministry. He was born in conformity with the prayerful revelations of the prophets (Isaiah 9: 6-7), lived and overcame temptations by complete reliance on prayer (Matthew 4: 1-11), ministered through the power of prayer (John 6: 11-12), confronted challenges with the weapon of prayer, was sustained during his hour of trials and darkness by the comfort of prayer (Luke 22: 39-41), and died on the cross praying, beseeching God to forgive his adversaries (Luke 23: 34).

Jesus considered regular, effectual, fervent conversation with God a necessity, and not an obligation. It was like blood and breath to him. He prayed with all that was in him and all that he had. When he prayed, his spirit, soul, and body were actively involved. He had faith in his heavenly father, constantly looked up to heaven, and was never disappointed by the One he trusted.

Thus, it is safe to say that prayer is one the greatest legacies of Jesus to his disciples as well as to all Christians. Not just as some empty acts of worship devoid of emotion to be recited, but a great calling to be highly coveted, deeply revered, and consciously embraced.

Those who have practiced praying from the heart, along with a body that was passionately engaged in the exercise, and a spirit that longed sincerely to connect with the spirit of God confess it is the most elevating, refreshing, and rewarding, experience any true believer can ever have.

IN MEMORY OF MY PARENTS

Sir Samuel Onyeuyo, and Lady Selina Chienyenwa

Who taught me to pray.

Epigraph

"Likewise the Spirit also helpeth our infirmities: for we know not what we should pray for as we ought: but the Spirit itself maketh intercession for us with groanings which cannot be uttered".

(Romans 8:26).

"And it came to pass, that, as he was praying in a certain place, when he ceased, one of his disciples said unto him, Lord, teach us to pray".

(Luke 11:1).

"Pray without ceasing".

(1 Thessalonians 5:17).

Chapter 1

WHAT IS PRAYER?

From the Christian perspective, prayer can be described as the flow of emotions that unites man with his God. It is that action by the natural man to identify with the sovereignty of the supernatural God through the humble demonstration of total submission to divine authority.

Prayer is an action often initiated from the natural realm by which a person declares allegiance to his maker who dwells in the spiritual plane. It is an indication of unalloyed loyalty by the created being to the creator of the universe, a symbol of rejection and renunciation of the authority of Satan over a life, or any of man's conscious or subconscious responses to that rare divine invitation that has the potential to kindle an enduring relationship with God. The act of prayer describes those moments in the exchange of emotion(s) when man and

God engage in intimate sacred interaction usually inspired by the urge to fellowship with one another.

Thus, prayer is evidence of human effort to make contact with the divine being, an act of man connecting with God through the power of words and feelings that bond the natural man with his supernatural God, as well as the fallen man's secret pathway to reconciliation through Christ, with a holy God.

In addition, prayer is that indispensable tool for evaluating the level of man's intimacy with God, as well as assessing the power of Christ in any life.

Difficult as the concept of prayer has been perceived, it is a process that surprisingly involves very simple, but disciplined habits which by regular practice can become beneficial reflex to those who engage in it.

Both bible accounts and extra biblical testimonies describe several incredible experiences of people like Abraham, Moses, Hannah, Daniel, Dr. Billy Graham, and Dr. Reinhardt Bonnke, to name a few, just because they prayed.

God excels through his virtues of loving kindness and mercy. And even when these attributes are said to dwell with him in the heavens, he still reaches out in his faithfulness to provide, sustain, protect, guide, guard, lead, and express himself in several gracious ways to those whose hearts are fixed on him through prayer. This was King David's conviction for which he declared:

> ***"Thy mercy, O Lord, is in the heavens: and thy faithfulness reacheth unto the clouds. Thy righteousness is like the great mountains: thy judgments are a great deep: O Lord, thou***

> ***preservest man and beast. How excellent is thy lovingkindness, O God! Therefore the children of men put their trust under the shadow of thy wings. They shall be abundantly satisfied with the fatness of thy house: and thou shall make them drink of the river of thy pleasures. For with thee is the fountain of life: in thy light shall we see light" (Psalms 36:5—9).***

The truth behind this observation makes it possible for man, even in the fallen state, to be reconnected to his source and "fountain", as he reaches out to God through acts of prayer. God is the light of all mankind. Without God and with no prayer, all life is condemned to darkness.

Prayer brings man into the presence of God, and through the exercise, the carnal man is able to catch a glimpse of supernatural events, perceive the mind of God, as well as enjoy several awesome, sometimes indescribable moments of divine glory.

Prayer may include the projection of our human thoughts, sighs, hopes, expectations, or wishes that may be tearfully expressed, sorrowfully vented, faithfully decreed, silently murmured, but preferably verbalized. All these are considered to be acts of prayer, as long as God is the focus. Thus, prayer can be described as:

1). The art of communicating with God.

Every community has a unique system by which it exchanges information within itself. It could be through signs, graphics, gestures, speech, or in writing, to meaningfully connect within that system, community or kingdom. For the believer in God and the Christian, prayer is the accepted means for that purpose. It is the major bridge through which the earthly person connects with his heavenly father.

The model prayer Jesus taught in the bible presents a unique pattern not only for ardent students in the school of prayer, but for all who desire to fellowship with God. This blueprint, among other vital tips, primarily shows the inevitable roles of God and man in sacred dialogue.

As will be observed in latter chapters concerning the how, why, what, where, and when of prayer, though its process can be initiated by man or by God, Jesus always opened the discussion, a practice that showed his unquestionable respect for God, total reliability on him, and complete subjection to his father's divine authority. King David also adopted this same pattern as reflected in the scripture:

> ***"O thou that hearest prayer, unto thee shall all flesh come" (Psalms 65:2).***

This was Jesus' secret code of reaching out to God. He always kick-started the prayer sessions, and taught his disciples to do same.

> ***"And he said unto them, when ye pray, say, Our Father which art in heaven" (Luke 11: 2).***

The candid submission to divine sovereignty, natural man's unashamed declaration of God's superiority, his honest admission of total dependence upon divine ability, are some of the defining characteristics that set the stage for that fulfilling encounter between the creator of all things, and the man he created for himself with the duty to worship him.

Jesus followed this simple, yet result oriented principle. He always put heaven in perspective first whenever he prayed, and trusted completely that God was more than ever ready to meet his request. He relied on God totally, and was never reluctant to show it as the records show in many instances:

> ***"And he commanded the multitude to sit down on the grass, and took the five loaves, and the two fishes, and looking up to heaven, he blessed, and brake, and gave the loaves to his disciples, and the disciples to the multitude" (Matthew 14: 19).***

> ***"Then they took away the stone from the place where the dead was laid. And Jesus lifted up his eyes, and said, Father, I thank thee that thou hast heard me" (John 11: 41).***

In every situation, Jesus never waited for God. He went to him first and always without hesitation.

2). Prayer is an act of worship.

Worship entails the sacred recognition of the divine nature of God, or the human response to Gods striking disclosure of himself through Christ. It is some act of appreciation of the revelation of God's will by a people, congregation, or person, and the acknowledgment of his invitation for fellowship. A celebration of this nature can take the form of songs, hymns, psalms, or choruses of praise that come deep down from the heart. It may involve the lifting up holy hands and hearts in honor of the almighty God who condescends to interact with ordinary mankind.

Thus, prayer of worship is any honest expression of human adoration of God, thanking him gratefully for his worthiness, and praising him for his immense goodness and mercy to all humanity.

While most human dialogues with the supernatural being focus mainly on needs and demands, the most satisfying initiative is that process embarked upon with only a deep hunger for divine intimacy. This type of worship sets out to acknowledge God just for who he is. This is the worship in spirit and truth that honors God, for it glorifies him for whom he has been, who he is, and shall remain forever.

However, while God demands and deserves our acts of worship, they cannot by any measure increase or diminish his nature and character. For no utterances, or imaginations of the carnal man are pure enough to honor God neither are any human actions fully sufficient to glorify him. Yet, it is every man's moral and spiritual duties to acknowledge God in worship for the awesomeness of his creation, part of which we all are.

This type of reverence quickly opens supernatural gates to the natural man, creating unhindered access to the courts of heaven and the heart of The Father, as such believer prays:

"Hallowed be thy name" (Luke 11: 2).

3). Prayer is conversation with God.

This type of conversation, as is fundamental with all dialogues, involves some verbal exchange between two or more people, this time, man and God. However, while the initiation of this process has been generally associated with man, it is God on the contrary, that originated the sacred concept of prayer.

> ***"And they heard the voice of the Lord God walking in the garden in the cool of the day: and Adam and his wife hid themselves from the presence of the Lord God amongst the trees of the garden. And the Lord God called out unto Adam, and said unto him, Where art thou? And he said, I heard thy voice in the garden, and I was afraid, because I was naked: and I hid myself" (Genesis 3:8-9).***

From the beginning, God has been the initiator of fellowship with man, even though the order over time became subsequently reversed as man began to enjoy the gains of the discipline to talk with God.

When prayer begins from the earthly realm, God listens while man speaks, and thereafter he responds.

> ***"In my distress I called upon the Lord, and cried unto my God: he heard my voice out of his temple, and my cry came before him, even into his ears". (Psalms 18: 6)***

> ***"Then the Lord answered Job out of the whirlwind, and said, Who is this that darkeneth counsel by words without knowledge? Gird up now thy loins like a man: for I will demand of thee, and answer me" (Job 38:1—3).***

In whichever case, God is the superior partner in the whole solemn exercise, which beyond every doubt leaves the other party involved with the reassuring feeling that God is near, and really cares.

> ***"Thus saith the Lord the maker thereof, the Lord that formed it, to establish it; the Lord is his name; Call unto me, and I will answer thee, and show thee great and mighty things, which thou knowest not" (Jeremiah 33: 2-3).***

So, God not only hears the one who prays, but condescends to respond even when sometimes the answer may not seem very satisfying.

4). Solemn but dynamic interaction with heaven.

Prayer is engaging in an obedient relationship with God that is built on absolute trust, awesome respect, and a deep hunger for fellowship. Unfortunately, the very vices of pride and rebellion that caused the fall of Adam and Eve in the Garden of Eden have not only kept mankind away from his God, but continued to deny him of the abundant benefits of a sweet covenant relationship with God. In addition, bad personal choices, perverse cultural changes, modern preferences for evil over good, and a satanically inspired urge to compromise the word of God have further soured what was meant to be an enviable relationship with the creator of the universe.

This has left man with a society that has little or no zeal to honor God, and no conscious intent to encounter him. And for the small segment of humanity that even wants to reconnect with God, the key principles that should make for easy and effective communication, have by religious conspiracy, been shrouded in some mystery claimed to be understood only by very "sanctified" and "anointed" few.

But thank God for this active and powerful medium which is still readily available, through his word, for the purpose of changing the dynamics of events in the lives of those who are genuinely hungry for that simple, sacred interaction with heaven.

> ***"For the word of God is quick, and powerful, and sharper than any two edged sword, piercing even to the dividing asunder of soul and spirit and of the joints and marrow, and is a discerner of the thoughts and intents of the heart" (Hebrews 4: 12).***

5). Persistent action before God.

There is always a huge difference when the natural man in fellowship with the supernatural God, presents an action plan relentlessly asking for favors, seeking for solutions, or knocking at the door of heaven concerning any problem. This manner of interaction, which in all essence reveals the lesser parties submission of inability to provide the required solution, always rewards the praying saint.

> ***"Ask, and it shall be given you; Seek, and ye shall find; Knock, and it shall be opened unto you" (Matthew 7:7).***

This is a fundamental principle that puts the inspired, dynamic, and lively word of God to test, and it usually has its reward.

Prayer is therefore, that vibrant, joyful, and persistent pursuit of God by man, or a man by his God.

6). Networking with heaven.

Prayer is an exchange between heaven and earth that is the entire time active within the spiritual communication network. It is a process that requires a steady and unobstructed line of conversation. This is where the prayer warrior excels most, because through this network he finds himself constantly in the presence of God thereby attracting priority attention.

According to the psalmist, God's presence offers direction, a life full of joy, and other innumerable pleasures to those who enter into it:

> ***"Thou wilt show me the path of life: in thy presence is fullness of joy: at thy right hand there are pleasures for evermore" (Psalms 16: 11).***

God is fully aware of all human needs, and goes ahead of man to address such desires even before they are presented to him. Yet, he demands that we pray concerning them.

> ***"And it shall come to pass, that before they call, I will answer; and while they are yet speaking, I will hear" (Isaiah 65:24).***

Prayer therefore is that determined effort by a person(s) to enter into the presence of God, and remaining there as much as possible.

7). Prayer is fellowship with God, in the name of Jesus.

The bible forbids any manner of fellowship that seeks to honor God in any name, spirit, angel, man or prophet, other than the name of Jesus. Even in the few Old Testament examples, where servants of prophets referenced their spiritual masters in their prayers, it was obvious they did not really pray in the name of those prophets, but evoked the name of the Lord God whom these masters served. In effect, they also honored Jesus while they prayed, even if they did not specifically mention his name.

> ***"And he took the mantle of Elijah that fell from him, and smote the waters, and said, Where is the Lord God of Elijah? and when he also had smitten the waters, they parted hither and thither: and Elisha went over" (2 Kings 2:14).***

Jesus said:

> ***"I am the Way, the Truth, and the Life: no man cometh unto the Father, but by me" (John 14:6).***

Praying in Jesus' name is the only sure way through which any petitioner can get into the presence of God. The name of Jesus opens supernatural doors. It is a name that is exalted and highly honored in heaven. So, given the right conditions, heaven goes on high alert when the prayer of faith knocks on the doors of God in the name of Jesus.

8). Prayer is inviting God into your battle.

Since the curse of God upon Adam and the serpent in the Garden of Eden, there has been active conflict between man, and the kingdom of darkness. This development explains why every believer will be engaged is some kind of spiritual warfare with unseen forces of darkness at some time or the other in a life time.

Most battles of life will not materialize physically because they are spiritual in nature and origin. As a result, they can neither be confronted with natural weapons, scientific devices, nor be adequately resolved by application of human force.

> ***"For though we walk in the flesh, we do not war after the flesh" (2Corinthians 10:3)***

The carnal man is a weak being by nature, so his human strategies cannot be adequate for confronting spiritual battles.

The good news however is that the God we serve, whose name is Jehovah, **"is a man of war"** (Exodus 15:3). As your battle is presented to God in prayer, he is able to deploy several invincible, spiritual weapons on your behalf which the devil and his agents cannot deal with. This is because prayer is the believer's most reliable means for attracting divine defense, as well as establishing his attack machine against the devil and all his works (2 Chronicles 20:1--15).

> ***"And he said, Harken ye, all Judah, and ye inhabitants of Jerusalem, and thou king Jehoshaphat, Thus saith the Lord unto you, Be not afraid nor dismayed by reason of this great multitude; for the battle is not yours, but God's. (2 Chronicles 20:15).***

The moment you surrender your life to Christ, the host of heaven begins to defend your interest while the Holy Spirit starts to employ weapons of warfare reserved only for the citizens of God's kingdom, on your behalf. These become your weapons of attack and amour of defense.

God is interested in your matter when you approach him concerning them through his word in prayer. The more scriptures you understand, employ, and apply to specific situations, the more victories you obtain in every battle you face.

Apostle Paul put it this way in his second epistle to the believers in Corinth:

> ***"(For the weapons of our warfare are not carnal, but mighty through God to the pulling down of strong holds): Casting down imaginations, and every high thing that exalteth itself against the knowledge of God, and bringing into captivity every thought to the obedience of Christ" (2Corinthian's 10:4-5).***

No action better describes the believer's hope of victory over an ugly situation more than a pious invitation of God through prayer into that circumstance.

9). Prayer is reminding God of his promises.

One of the major objectives of prayer is to remind God of his promises. However, every of God's promises for man is guided by conditions provided for in some covenant arrangement. It is important to note that every covenant has four parts: 1) The parties involved. 2) The conditions of the agreement. 3) The promises of the agreement, and 4) The seal of the covenant.

Through the process of prayer a person can get back to God to demand for, or claim his pledge, after fulfilling the conditions set out in the contract. God never forgets his promise; rather he follows his word to perform every promise of his covenant.

> ***"For God is not a man that he would lie, nor the son of man that he would repent. Has he said it and will he not bring it to pass?" (Numbers23:19).***

The story of Caleb is a vivid illustration here. As one of the twelve spies who brought back a positive report from spying the land of Canaan, by the divine commission of Moses, God rewarded Caleb's steadfast loyalty by ensuring that he survived the wilderness death that wiped out his generation. Caleb was also allotted a special heritage in the region of Hebron, in the Promised Land. When God pronounced this promise, Caleb was only forty years old. Forty five years later, it had not come to pass. But Caleb was relentless, for he knew that if God said it, he would perform it.

> ***"Then the children of Judah came unto Joshua in Gilgal: and Caleb the son of Jephunneh the Kenezite said to him, Thou knowest the thing that the Lord said unto Moses the man of God concerning me and thee in Kadesh Barnea. Forty years old was I when the servant of the Lord sent me from Kadesh Barnea to espy out the land; and I brought him word again as it was in my heart. Nevertheless my brethren that went up with me made the heart of the people melt: but I wholly followed the Lord my God. And Moses sware on that day, saying, Surely the land whereon thy feet have trodden shall be thine inheritance, and thy children's forever, because thou hast wholly followed the Lord thy God" (Joshua 14: 6—8).***

With this confidence, Caleb approached Joshua who was God's mouth piece for Israel at the time, took him up on this promise, and through Joshua, God expedited his vow to Caleb.

> ***"Now therefore give me this mountain, whereof the Lord spake in that day; for thou heardest in that day how the Anakims were there, and that the cities were great and fenced; if so be the Lord will be with me, then I shall be able to drive them out as the Lord said. And Joshua blessed him, and gave unto Caleb the***

> ***son of Jephunneh Hebron for an inheritance" (Joshua 14: 12—13).***

As the believer calls God to remembrance concerning any promise he has spoken, God always rises to the challenge. Tying God to his word justifies the petition as well as the petitioner.

10). Prayer is applying God's word to obtain his blessing.

Every favor obtained from God is already enshrined in his word. Your prayer is like the moisture that softens the ground, while the request is the seed. As relevant scriptures are evoked over specific needs, strongholds crumble, mountains are moved, tests become testimonies, trials lead the way to triumph and answers to questions begin manifest without restraint.

Divine favors, like all treasures are hidden riches that can only be found in deep places. They are there, but nonetheless buried beneath the earth. Those who find them do so by digging real deep, and with the right instruments. So goes with finding God's favor, a truth supported by scripture as recorded by King Solomon:

> ***"It is the glory of God to conceal a thing: but the honor of kings to reveal it" (Proverbs 25:2).***

Moses, the prophet of God put it this way:

> ***"The secret things belong unto the Lord our God: but those things which are revealed***

> ***belong unto us and to our children forever, that we may do all the words of the law" (Deuteronomy29: 29).***

Through constant interaction with God and the right application of his word, mysteries concealed in time can be assessed.

The word of God has power to reveal mysteries. That is why those who want to obtain God's blessings must apply God's word.

11). Prayer is dialogue in the language of heaven.

Every community of people, culture, kingdom, or nations, has a peculiar means by which those within that system interact among themselves. God is a living, speaking creature who spoke the entire universe and all that is in it into being by the power of his word (Genesis 1: 1—31).

Prayer is what happens as man in the natural realm begins to connect with the Triune persons in the supernatural sphere through the living word. It could be through the cries of bitterness, moaning of grief, sighs of anguish, exclamation of joy, shout of victory and any other means that man employs, or it could be man striving to understand the signs by which God expresses himself, as with Moses in the burning bush, for the purpose of revelation and instruction, or to Elijah in a still small voice, for divine reassurance.

> ***"And the Angel of the Lord appeared unto him in a flame of fire out of the midst of a bush: and he looked, and, behold, the bush burnt with fire, and the bush was not consumed.***

> ***And Moses said, I will now turn aside, and see this great sight, why the bush is not burnt. And when the Lord saw that he turned aside to see, God called unto him out of the midst of the bush, and said, Moses, Moses. And he said. Here am I. And he said. Draw not nigh hither: put off thy shoes from off thy feet, for the place whereon thou standest is holy ground. Moreover he said, I am the God of thy father, the God of Abraham, the God of Isaac, and the God of Jacob. And Moses hid his face; for he was afraid to look upon God" (Exodus 3: 2—6).***

Understanding the language of heaven is prerequisite for effective communication and communion with God. It facilitates human interaction with the divine. This knowledge of the word and language of heaven gives character to prayer, and deepens our worship. The devil and his family of demons cannot understand it, therefore they cannot pray.

12). Prayer is the natural linking up with the supernatural.

Much as God is faithful and kind, he will not unilaterally meddle into many circumstances until you invite him. It is your prerogative to let him in, or shut him out of any situation in your life.

Those who desire to get in touch with God must ensure that the channel of interaction between them will not by any means be obstructed either by carnal distractions, or spiritual communication defects. Their spiritual antennae must be fine-tuned to very alert mode that enables clear reception of signals from the divine network of frequencies that exist between earth and heaven.

Nothing worthwhile can actually be achieved without divine approval. It is by heaven's intervention that anyone can prosper without unnecessary struggle, which explains why every believer should establish this very important link with God.

Every human creature will at some time or the other have a dire need that will call for the imminent attention of heaven, an instance that will require dependence on the power and person of God.

In Jacob's situation, it was this kind of experience that led him, in mid-life, to completely surrender his carnal struggles and dubious character to God at Abraham's altar of prayer in Bethel, where also he rededicated himself to God's covenant (Genesis 28: 10-22).

So, a time will come when no one can afford a life without a living altar of prayer dedicated to the Most High God.

PRAYER POINTS.

1). O Lord, strengthen me to pray without ceasing, in Jesus name.

2). Holy Spirit, help me to develop an attitude of humility in prayer, in Jesus name.

3). O Lord, when I pray hear, and answer me quickly, in Jesus name.

4). My father, let my prayers be acceptable to you, in Jesus name.

5). Lord Jesus, connect me to the presence of God through your shed blood, in Jesus name.

6). Holy Spirit, keep my network with heaven always clear, in Jesus name.

7). My prayers shall attract divine attention, in Jesus name.

8). I shall not pray in vain, no matter the circumstance, in Jesus name.

9). Where-ever my matter is mentioned, Lord Jesus, stand as my advocate, in Jesus name.

10). My prayers shall attract angelic assistance, in Jesus name.

Chapter 2

WHY PRAY?

"When the stakes are high, bow down low".
(Beth Moore)

1). The times are evil.

We live in times that are very evil, with uncommon and unusual events occurring as if they were normal. Cycles of disaster are showing up concurrently at different regions of the world with overwhelming rapidity. All over the continents, forest fires, flash floods, earthquakes, landslides, violent tornadoes are claiming lives and sweeping away property. Suicides, homicides, abductions, rape, murder, are on the increase. Abortions can now be readily obtained at street corners in many so called advanced countries, with government funding and approval, even so with certain classified drugs.

On the economic sector, the spending power of most families is fast shrinking, while poverty, hunger, prostitution, infant mortality, and age-induced sicknesses are on the sharp rise. In China, North Korea, Iran, Iraq, Afghanistan, Pakistan, and most countries of Africa, there is so much human and religious rights abuse. The internecine conflicts in the troubled ancient kingdoms of the Middle-East sub region have caused that zone to be perceived, rightly or wrongly, as the most unstable place to live on earth, and the political time bomb of this generation.

In the United States, as well as in most countries of South America, more people are shot and killed on the streets from guns, drugs, and alcohol related incidents than in the war in Afghanistan. Marital homes are unstable, and there are more single-parent families now than in the generations past. Divorce rate is on the increase even amongst people of faith, while evil moral choices, for which God judged the generation of Noah, and punished the nations of Sodom, Gomorrah, Admah, and Zeboiim, are on the steep rise.

In this generation, subjects biblically classified as abominations, have suddenly become issues of public ridicule that are backed by Government, and surprisingly endorsement by the political class in our so-called modern society. Moral guards have outrageously been let down, and social values once treated with fear and trembling are daily being violated by even those who should protect them.

Today, God's righteous standards, which once formed the pillars of socio-cultural and political fabrics of many nations, and shaped the characters of their founding fathers, have been derided, redefined, and debased. And while the devil and his cronies are celebrating in their print and electronic media, the church is watching bemused.

Our generation has become the age that drinks iniquity like water; a society so sick from spiritual and moral decay that the less garment covering human body parts, the higher the fashion rating in society. This is the tragedy of the times, a sad situation that can only be remedied by nothing else, but **Prayer**.

2). Jesus prayed.

Jesus was born during the troubled era in bible history when gross superstition, social chaos, intellectual ignorance, complicated religious practices, and abject lack of the true knowledge of the word of God was the norm.

So, from the beginning of his ministry, the simple message of repentance he preached (Matthew 4:17), the intimate fellowship he enjoyed through prayer with his father, coupled with his better understanding of God's will for his kingdom confounded many of the religious leaders of his time who supposedly were the custodians of the Law. Before long, that simple message, backed by many undeniable miracles Jesus worked, began to resonate with the people. The result was that many of the publicans as well as a few high placed Pharisees "caught the fire", without realizing the secret.

But the secret of Jesus' success was nothing more than prayer, prayer, and more prayer that transcended traditional practices and cultural preferences, in the quest for God. Jesus was in constant touch with God. He prayed all the time, everywhere, and over everything. In certain and uncertain places (Luke 11: 1), for the demon possessed (Mark 5: 1-10), at the tomb of Lazarus (John 11:38), over meals (Matthew 26:27), on the sea of Galilee (Matthew 8:23-27), before sunrise, for his disciples (John 17: 1-26), at night (Luke 22:53), while alone (Matthew 26:36), when with others (Luke 22: 39-45), on the cross (Luke 23: 46), and even for those who perceived him as their enemy (Luke 23: 11). He prayed passionately, and relentlessly; sometimes in tears (John 11:35), many times with compassion (Matthew 15:32-37), and other times in agony (Luke 22: 44; 23: 44; Mark 14: 33-35).

In like manner, Jesus taught his disciples to pray (Luke 11:1-4), a lesson which Apostle Paul re-affirmed in his first epistle to the church in Thessalonica during which he admonished them to: **"Pray without ceasing" (1 Thessalonians 5:17).**

3). To acknowledge God's existence.

> ***"The fool has said in his heart there is no God"***
> (Psalms 14:1).

Prayer is admitting the reality of divine existence, the truth of which is made more apparent by the overwhelming awe of God's glorious manifestation during most such exercises. For no power outside the divine influence is able to arouse such sublime flow of emotion in the natural man, other than his maker with whom he shares the same spirit.

The creator of the entire universe is our God, and his name is Jehovah. As he is reverenced through prayer, the soul so engaged is overcome by an initial burst of godly fear that soon eases into an elated feeling of joy, peace, and happiness. In this state of mind, the natural man has sometimes been privileged to perceive divine transactions, and catch rare glimpses of the beauty, splendor, wonder, and majesty of God in his supernatural realm, which are divinely prohibited from human description. Apostle Paul's personal experience was recorded in his second letter to the Corinthians like this:

> ***"I knew a man in Christ above fourteen years ago, (whether in the body, I cannot tell: or whether out of the body, I cannot tell: God knoweth): such an one caught up to the third heaven. And I knew such a man, (whether in the body, or out of the body, I cannot tell: God knoweth): How that he was caught up into paradise, and heard unspeakable words, which it is not lawful for a man to utter" (2 Corinthians 12: 2—4).***

Only the fool says there is no God. In reality, many people have encountered God, and relished very awesome experiences which deniers of his existence are not privileged to enjoy.

> ***"The fool hath said in his heart, There is no God. Corrupt are they, and have done abominable iniquity: there is none that doeth good" (Psalms 53:1).***

That Christian whose prayer is to the living God is sure to experience him in one form or the other someday.

4). To evoke divine awareness.

Several examples from the bible describe people who were overcome by the joyous sensation of divine glory while in the serene attitude of prayer. However, while this "Shechinah" loves to dwell with God's people, it is mainly in times of prayer that its manifest influence is reasonably felt. The prophet Daniel was so overwhelmed by one such exerting, but nonetheless, exhilarating glorious experience he could hardly stand on his feet (Daniel 10: 10—12).

As soon as a fervent prayer session is initiated, an instant aura of divine awareness overshadows the person, congregation, and or environment so engaged. It is an incomprehensible, yet tangible cloud of emotion that is evidence of supernatural influence upon the sacred moment of fellowship. This spiritual energy inherent in the concept of prayer is the very essence of inspired worship. It is responsible for enabling the appropriate conditions that open doors for visions and revelations, in addition to emboldening the one praying, as he effectually exercises his divine prerogative.

The Christian does not serve an absentee god, but a living, spiritual being that is ever present, and so mindful of his children that he constantly reaches out to interact with them.

Howbeit, while it is God's good pleasure to open his door of fellowship to mankind, it is man's responsibility on the other hand to adequately prepare through the righteousness of Christ, to enter into his throne room for such glorious encounter.

5). To interact with God.

According to the psalmist, the believer can experience an over-flowing stream of joy by remaining in the presence of God.

> ***"Thou will show me the path of life: in thy presence is fullness of joy, at thy right hand there are pleasures for evermore"*** (Psalms 16:11).

The secret of God's abundant treasures are mainly revealed in times of undistracted, patient endurance before his presence. It is during such moments of solitude that endowed spiritual gifts are activated, callings received, and divine assignments commissioned.

Being in God's presence helps remove all aberrations that would humanly clog a person's clear perception in the natural realm, sharpen human senses, and increase natural appreciation for spiritual realities. These are few of the benefits of being constantly pre-occupied with God in prayer. No one can lose by praying, because it is the one thing that is able to dismantle the human limits consciously or unconsciously placed between man and God.

6). To understand the mind of God.

While no natural man can thoroughly understand the mind of God, the concept of prayer particularly at the levels of worship and meditation, helps the soul of the spiritually minded person to connect and be in harmony with his spirit of God. As the Apostle Paul stated in his letter to the Colossians, the Christian is to:

> ***"Set your affection on things above, not on things on the earth" (Colossians 3:2).***

The carnal man whose prayer is based on the spiritual word enjoys the rare privilege of perceiving God's voice as well as being able to discern his will. As this practice becomes habit, accompanied with growth in divine knowledge and the obedient application of supernatural truth, an intimate relationship develops between such a person and God. This deep bond of affection can only be sustained as such a believer lives in the constant renewal of their natural mind through the nourishment of the spiritual word of prayer.

> ***"And be not conformed to this world: but be ye transformed by the renewing of your mind, that ye may prove what is that good, and acceptable, and perfect will of God (Romans 12:2).***

Knowing the mind of God can help a regenerated person to fashion his soul according to God's mindset. This is how a Christian can begin to conform to the divine image of his creator.

7). To humbly contend with Heaven.

Abraham and Moses are two examples that illustrate how possible it is for a child of God to reasonably argue their case with him, without making a ridicule of oneself. They employed the medium of prayer, and in a very humble manner laid out their matter before God.

To reason with God is a favor which all Christians can enjoy. It is a divine privilege reserved for his faithful and bold children who know their rights and demand these of God. These are the real joint heirs with Jesus Christ who know the promises of God for their lives, and how to apply the word of God to obtain them.

The contending prayer however is not an instrument for blind arguments, but a tool of appeal for mercy, even in conditions where condemnation is most deserved.

For instance, in Abraham's appeal to God for the exoneration of his nephew from the judgment upon Sodom and Gomorrah, he did not make any blind assumptions concerning Lot's righteousness; neither did he rely on emotional human sentiments about his relationship with God. He was undoubtedly God's trusted friend (Genesis 18: 17-18), yet he chose this very approach in his intercession for Lot. He respectfully argued his case.

> ***"And Abraham drew near, and said, Wilt thou also destroy the righteous with the wicked? Peradventure there be fifty righteous within the city; wilt thou also destroy and not spare the place for the fifty righteous that are therein? That be far from thee to do after this manner, to slay the righteous with the wicked, and that the righteous should be as the wicked; that be far from thee: Shall not the* Judge *of all the earth do right?"*** (Genesis 18: 23-25).

Abraham persuasively engaged God in this discussion urging him to spare the evil city, not for the fact that he loved Sodom or her sins, but in order to save his righteous nephew, Lot who dwelt there.

> ***"And the Lord said, if I find in Sodom fifty righteous within the city, then I will spare all the place for their sakes."*** (Genesis 18: 26)

This is what the prayer of contention is all about. It is a form of litigation argued with all humility and supporting facts in the courts of God.

In the same manner, Moses prayed to God in the wilderness concerning the children of Israel. The children of Israel had generally become rebellious, with several leaders of families compulsively murmuring against God's constituted authority, and in-sighting riot in the camp. This transgression drew the anger of God, and when he threatened to consume them in his wrath, Moses intervened, reasoning with his heart of mercy (Numbers 16:1--21).

You can appeal to God in any situation to your favor by taking hold of the relevant scripture(s). In such circumstances, God very much honors his word as he honors his name.

Abraham and Moses respectively did this and caused significant changes to what was supposed to God's intended action. Their intervention in that moment of prayer made the difference. You too can learn from them by boldly, but respectfully, going into the court-room of God to obtain mercy for yourself and for others, or to defer justice.

8). To expropriate the power in the word of God.

Words have power, particularly the word of God, and can make a huge difference in a person's life depending on how they are applied. Whatever success is enjoyed today can be traced to the words spoken in the past. Negative words spoken in the past can hold a person's present and future hostage. That is why it is important to regularly and positvely speak God's word in faith, as this will lead to unlimited success in future.

To speak God's word, is to command it, decree it, or declare it with authority. God's word in your mouth is as powerful a tool as it is in his own. The world was created simply by the power of the spoken word of God. He spoke, and the things that were not previously in existence came into being as if they already had existed. This is the power in the spoken word.

There is awesome power in righteous words, tremendous power enough to connect a person to the socket of unimaginable success, while aligning those whose words are wicked or indecent to the power house of failure. There is power in the confessions you make today sufficient to favor your destiny in the future.

In psalms number 23, David made a very great proclamation that aligned with the word of God. He refused to let the devil employ the strategy of fear to destroy his faith in God. Fear can come in the form of dark shadows that imprison a believer's soul, eroding their faith in God.

Life can be fraught with challenges like David experienced. But despite those dark shadows, the Christian must decline the temptation to be subdued by the power of fear. Instead, he is encouraged to confront any ugly situation with boldness of faith leaning to God in the manner that David did praying:

> ***"Yea, though I walk through the valley of the shadow of death, I will fear no evil: for thou art with me; thy rod and thy staff, they comfort me"*** (Psalms 23:4).

David refused to be scared by the frightening shadows of death, claiming the protection of God's rod and staff. So, even in the face of imminent defeat, learn to trust God in prayer, and his words you confess will bring you unexpected victory.

Praying the word of God has innumerable benefits. It presumes the one doing so knows God's desire, and is willing to abide by it. When this is the case, that believer can be sure to enjoy a prosperous life as these scriptures state:

> ***"My son, forget not my law; but let thine heart keep my commandments: For length of days, and long life, and peace, shall they add to thee" (Proverbs 3:2).***

> ***"He sent his word, and healed them, and delivered them from their destructions" (Psalms 107:20).***

Pray like this:

"O Lord, let your word that has gone forth, bring me healing and deliverance, in Jesus' name."

> ***"When the wicked, even my enemies and my foes, came upon me to eat up my flesh, they stumbled and fell".*** (Psalms 27:2)

Pray like this:

"Weapons of the wicked, prepared to destroy my life, destroy your owner, in Jesus' name."

"O Lord, make the path of my wicked pursuers dark and slippery, in Jesus name."

9). To initiate divine beneficial changes.

There is no situation that cannot be resolved through prayer. The testimony of Prophet Daniel is sound evidence that prayer can change any situation. No one gets thrown into a den of lions and comes out alive, except in the celebrated case of Daniel, the man of prayer (Daniel 6:11—22).

When Apostle Paul and Silas, his traveling companion, were cast into the Philippian jail, they resorted to prayer and praise until the prison walls began to shake from their foundations (Philippians 16:21-24). Prayer will turn your darkness into light, your rags to riches, and take you from the valley of reproach to the mountain top of celebration.

After Moses prayed for forty days and nights at the top of Mount Sinai, no one could look on his face, because the brightness of God's glory was upon him. This brightness of divine glory set him apart, and changed the way his brethren regarded him from then on.

In the bible account of the Transfiguration of Jesus, the cosmic events surrounding the entire event, confirm the power of prayer. Whenever God is in the picture, circumstances change as we pray.

> ***"And it came to pass about an eight days after these sayings, he took Peter, and John, and James, and went up into a mountain to pray. And as he prayed, the fashion of his countenance was altered, and his raiment was white and glistering. And behold, there talked with him two men, which were Moses and Elias. Who appeared in glory, and spake of the decease which he should accomplish at Jerusalem" (Luke 9: 28-31).***

The change in Jesus' outlook and the brightness of his garment all occurred while he prayed. Prayer will change a life.

It will transform the character of weakness in an individual into one of strength, turn demotion into promotion, and cause imminent defeat become resounding victory. It will open closed doors of favor, remove mountains, restore hope, turn mourning into laughter, and set captives free.

There is God's anointing and power in prayer to change things; to bring light that will disperse darkness, hope to overcome despair, healing in place of sickness, and deliverance in every area of bondage. As you pray in Jesus name, you can be sure to achieve the impossible, and turn the table against your enemies.

10). Prayer creates the right atmosphere for divine manifestation.

Testimonies are conceived in the womb of prayer. Looking up to heaven through the lenses of God's living word brings remarkable transformations in the life of any believer. Through prayer, the carnal man can receive approval for divine assignment and anointing to live a consecrated life.

> ***"And there came a voice out of the cloud, saying, This is my beloved Son, hear him".***
> (Luke 9:35).

Jesus special authority as the Messiah who will fulfill both the law and the prophets was divinely confirmed on this occasion as Moses and Elijah fellowshipped with him in prayer.

Each believer has a unique purpose in life that heaven is anxiously waiting to endorse. But there has to be surrender to God through prayer, and the same God that testified of Jesus'

Sonship will do the same for everyone who prays to fulfill their own divine purpose.

11). Prayer invokes the Blessings of God.

Nothing opens the doors of God's blessings wider than prayer. It is the surest way to dispatch reproach from a life, remove the garment of affliction, and invite joy and laughter into a contrite and broken life.

Abraham was seventy five years old when God promised him a child by Sarah. He never gave up his hope for this blessing, but kept his expectation alive with relentless pleas to God which resulted in the birth of Isaac by Sarah, his wife. He was then almost hundred years old. The miraculous birth of Isaac was nothing but the result of several years of prayer.

Hannah too was childless. Then one year, as she went up with her husband Elkanah and sister-in-law Peninnah to the annual religious feast in Shiloh, she invoked God's blessing upon her life, tying her request to a vow. Thereafter, God answered her, she conceived by her husband Elkanah, and gave birth to a son named Samuel who was a great prophet in Israel (1 Samuel 1:1-20).

Apostle Peter's miraculous release from Herod's prison in Jerusalem, was due to the incessant prayer of the church unto God for him (Acts 12:5-17). The same goes for Apostles Paul and Silas, whose violent prayer and praise not only brought about their un-common deliverance from prison, but resulted in the conversion of the keeper of the prison and his entire house-hold (Acts 16:16-40).

When a Christian prays, he receives divine relief as his prayers cause the cloud of blessing to release its rain into his situation.

PRAYER POINTS.

1). Holy Spirit, embrace me with your ever abiding presence, in Jesus name.
2). O Lord, give me a consuming passion for your kingdom, in Jesus name.
3). My father, hide me under the shadow of your wings, in Jesus name.
4). O Lord, give me the ability to think clearly, boldness to speak freely, and power to act truthfully, in Jesus name.
5). O Lord, make me to carry your banner without shame, in Jesus name.
6). The confidence of the wicked over my life shall disappoint them, in Jesus name.
7). Holy Spirit, turn the words of my petition into the language of heaven, in Jesus name.
8). O God arise, and turn my night of mourning into my day of joy, in Jesus name.
9). O Lord, clothe me with the garment of your glory, in Jesus name.
10). Thou rock of my defense, do not forsake me, in Jesus name.

Chapter 3

Types of Prayer.

There are different varieties of prayer, just as experiences in life differ. One kind of prayer definitely may not be suitable in a different circumstance. The motivation for prayer often determines the most relevant style to adopt. Any of the various types can be employed by itself, or in combination with the others. However, while prayer in the general context serves the same purpose, one type of prayer remarkably differs from the other as we shall see below.

1). Prayer of Confession and Repentance.

According to David Roper, in his book, "Psalm 23-The Song Of A Passionate Heart", ***"Humility and contrition are the keys to the heart of God***". But true as this statement stands, the ideas of confession and repentance are two of the most difficult elements of prayer to propagate, as they so often imply the acceptance of guilt, committal of some offence, or rebellion against God's law. However, those who understand the importance of confession and repentance in the concept of prayer agree that it is fundamental in the process of reconciliation with God.

As is clearly shown in King David's humble contrition after the awful Bathsheba saga, honest confession and humble repentance hold the key to reconciliation with God. For no one can experience the restoring power of God's love and forgiveness except they enter through the gates of true confession and genuine repentance.

> ***"Have mercy upon me, O God, according to thy loving kindness: according unto the multitude of thy tender mercies blot out my transgressions. Wash me thoroughly from my iniquity, and cleanse me from my sin. For I acknowledge my transgressions: and my sin is ever before me" (Psalms 51:1-3).***

> ***"For thou desirest not sacrifice: else would I give it: thou delightest not in burnt offering. The sacrifices of God are a broken spirit: a broken and a contrite heart, O God, thou wilt not despise" (Psalms51:16-17).***

God is the head of a righteous judicial system that operates over his kingdom. This system functions effectively through human obedience to the laws of God. The believer who falls short of the requirements of God's commandment, but becomes regretful of his action, can take his case to the court of God, confess such sins, forsake them, and obtain forgiveness and mercy. This process of confession to obtain pardon can only be achieved through acts of prayer.

The blood of Jesus is so saturated with forgiveness that any penitent sinner can be cleansed, be reconciled with God, and receive grace and mercy for restoration in fellowship.

Those who worship God with unrepentant heart make a mockery of prayer. Such prayers are referred to as abomination, and do not receive any attention in heaven as confirmed by this scripture:

> ***"If I regard iniquity in my heart, the Lord will not hear me"*** (Psalms 66: 18).

Thus, a good place to start for anyone who seriously intends to fellowship with God is at the point of acknowledgment and confession of all known sins.

The next step is the level of repenting from, and forsaking of those sins. This whole process involves accepting full responsibility for the person's sins, the iniquity of their parents and grand- parents, as well as all ancestral abominations back to several generations (Exodus 20: 5). An honest Christian prayer acknowledges these sins, humbly confesses them, and remorsefully condemns these transgressions. All humans bear the nature of the fallen man, Adam. It is the confession of this sin and the acceptance of Christ's redemptive work that reconciles man again with God.

> ***"if we say we have no sin, we deceive ourselves and the truth is not in us. If we confess our sins,***

> ***he is faithful and just to forgive us our sins, and to cleanse us from all unrighteousness" (1 John 1: 8-9).***

Confession and repentance are therefore the recommended starting blocks on the platforms of prayer. They form the strong foundation upon which some kinds of prayers must be built.

2). Prayer of Adoration. (Matthew 6:9-10; Revelations 4:11).

Adoration is the celebration of the majesty of God and the beauty of his holiness. It is that sublime attitude of surrender of the spirit, soul, and body in declaration of his worthiness, acknowledging his authority, ascribing power and might to his majesty, and appreciating him for his unique nature and character. It is engaging in that deep, unreserved devotion to express the awesomeness of God through recalling the unimaginable attributes and virtues that set him apart, and make him worthy of worship.

The prayer of adoration involves the verbal, joyful admiration in praise acknowledging the Sovereign God by the different titles through which he revealed himself, some of which include: "The eternal God", "The King of kings", "The Lord of lords", "The "I Am that I Am", "The Bright and Morning Star". "The Lion of the tribe of Judah", "The Rock of Ages", "Ancient of days", "The Alpha and Omega", "The invincible God", "The all sufficient One", the God that is worthy of praise. Halleluiah!!!!!!!

The psalmist adopted this method in his dealings with God as can be observed in the following scriptures:

> ***"O Lord our Lord, how excellent is thy name in all the earth! Who hast set thy glory above the heavens" (Psalms 8:1).***

> ***"When I consider thy heavens, the work of thy fingers the moon and the stars, which thou has ordained. What is man, that thou art mindful of him? and the son of man, that thou visited him?"*** (Psalms 8:3-4)

> ***"For thou hast made him a little lower than the angels, and has crowned him with glory and honor" (Psalms 8:5).***

> ***"Thou madest him to have dominion over the works of thy hands; thou hast put all things under his feet" (Psalms 8:6).***

Moses' victory song after God overthrew Pharaoh and the Egyptians in the Red sea was also a prayer of adoration:

> ***"Who is like unto thee, O Lord, among the gods? Who is like thee, glorious in holiness, fearful in praises, doing wonders?" (Exodus 15:11).***

This is a solemn devotion in high admiration of God with all due respect. It is identifying with God's indisputable power, and humbly submitting to his protective strength in the light of human weakness. The prayer of adoration gives the carnal man the opportunity to declare his unworthiness while admitting the steadfast love of the faithful God.

The glory of God almighty often overwhelms that genuine Christian who in all honesty of purpose and sincerity of heart finds fulfilling joy whilst lost in the maze of divine adoration. This is a great medium of interaction with heaven.

3). Liquid Prayer.

When the stakes are high, the Christian must not be shy to cry. Clinging to anxiety, stress, grief, un-forgiveness and any type of bitterness will lead to the "hard heart" syndrome. This is a spiritual disease suffered by those who carry un-necessary burden. But healing can come as these emotions are released through your holy cry. The scripture recommends taking the tears to God where one will find the needed comfort (Matthew 11:28).

The concept of the liquid prayer is commonly associated with the cry of a desperate soul. It is usually the last option of a desperate life in despair. Many have been caught in this kind of circumstance where the last source of comfort was the Holy Spirit.

The liquid prayer is an outpouring of a broken heart, an emotional, but justifiable, outburst of inaudible sobs of surrender to God that speak more eloquently than tongues.

Liquid prayer may result from the passionate outcry of a hurting soul, or can be the outpouring of an overwhelmed heart in thanksgiving to his Awesome God. Whichever is the case, it is the powerful expression of a subdued heart praying more than words can declare.

When the children of Israel cried to God on account of their suffering in Egypt, God responded immediately.

> ***"Now therefore, behold, the cry of the children of Israel is come unto me: and I have also seen the oppression wherewith the Egyptians oppress them. Come now therefore, and I will send thee unto Pharaoh, that thou mayest bring forth my people the children of Israel out of Egypt" (Exodus 3: 9-10).***

There is righteous grief in tears that instantly connects to godly compassion, and attracts divine attention.

So, while some may consider the act of crying a sign of weakness, heaven never overlooks the holy out-pouring of a broken and contrite heart. The bitter tears shed on the altar of prayer often evoke the compassion of our loving God because they are usually cries in desperation.

There will always be a time to weep, whether the uncontrollable tears of joy or the agonizing cry of hardship, disappointment, wretchedness or grief. When the need arises, do not be shy to cry to God. Even our Lord Jesus Christ wept when he had the reason to do so (John 11:35).

The song by King David at the dedication of his house and inauguration of his reign reveals what can happen when a person sheds solemn tears of penitence, complaint, or of request at the prayer altar:

> ***"For his anger endureth but a moment; in his favor is life: weeping may endure for a night, but joy cometh in the morning" (Psalms 30:5).***

This was also Hannah's approach which in the end yielded divine relief.

> ***"And she was in bitterness of soul, and prayed unto the Lord, and wept sore" (1 Samuel1:10).***

This is a very effective method of reaching out to God, especially when the agony and tears represent the total surrender of human hopeless to an able God.

This is what is meant by liquid prayer.

4). Prayer of Thanksgiving. (Philippians 4: 6).

Thanksgiving is a show of gratitude directed at God for all his blessings. While many regard the celebration of divine goodness as a festive event reserved only for certain seasons, the bible teaches that the appreciation of the graces of God ought to be a way of life, a routine attitude to be engaged in with joy.

In Apostle Paul's letter to the believers in Ephesus, he emphasized this need to give thanks at all times for all things:

> ***"Giving thanks always for all things unto God and the Father in the name of our Lord Jesus Christ" (Ephesians 5:20).***

All you are, can ever be, or possess, are due to the grace of God. No one deserves these, neither does any merit them. That is why the believer must develop the humble attitude of thanksgiving.

Thanksgiving must represent the believer's genuine acknowledgement of God's sufficiency despite human unworthiness. It ought to be the sincere, outward show of gratitude to God for his ability and willingness to meet all of mankind's teeming needs. In other words, it is thanking God for being there for you, and caring the way no one else would do. It is admitting the futility of human ability, and recognizing that man is helpless and hopeless without God.

The prayer of thanksgiving while expressing gratitude for what God has done, can also be a demonstration of faith in him for expectations that are yet to be fulfilled. However, it must be noted that it pleases God when one prays with gratitude for petitions that did not turn out the way expected.

Thus, it is worth the while to spend valuable time in prayer, thanking God for each day. Appreciate him with words that make sweet music to the ears of heaven, for hardly will anyone reject honest and true expression of praise and appreciation. When you honor God for his kindness he opens the doors of heaven giving you more reasons to be thankful.

5). Prayer of Supplication

This form of prayer is devotion in earnest petition to God for help. The believer inspired to pray in this manner reaches out to God, passionately pleading, and humbling entreating him for a favorable response. Nevertheless, while supplication calls for relentlessness, its model presumes that God is not only willing, but able to intervene on behalf of the petitioner if only they will persist. God is moved by the believer's prayer of supplication because it is a practice he usually adopts in dealing with his children when necessary, as we see in this scripture:

> ***"Thus saith thy Lord the Lord, and thy God that pleaded the cause of his people, Behold, I have taken out of thine hand the cup of trembling, even the dregs of the cup of my fury, thou shall no more drink it again: But I will put it into the hand of them that afflict thee:***

> ***which have said to thy soul, Bow down, that we may go over: and thou has laid thy body as the ground, and as the street, to them that went over" (Isaiah 51:22-23).***

The Apostle Paul encourages Christians not to allow the cares and worries of life to hinder them when they pray, but rather to engage in relentless pleading with God, a practice which ushers in a peace that comes from knowing that God is in control of the situation.

> ***"Be careful for nothing, but in everything by prayer and supplication, with thanksgiving let your let your requests be made known unto God. And the peace of God, which passeth all understanding, shall keep your hearts and minds through Christ Jesus". (Philippians 4:6).***

The more confident you are that God hears and answers prayers, the more challenged you are to pray until he responds. And the more you pray, the less you will worry about issues irrespective of their size, source, and nature.

6). Prayer of Intercession. (Daniel 9: 1-19).

God is looking for intercessors for the nations, and for his people. Unfortunately, there are not many who are willing to respond to this call.

> ***"And I sought for a man among them that should make up the hedge, and stand in the***

gap before me for the land, that I should not destroy it: but I found none". (Ezekiel 22:30).

Intercessors are believers that have burden for perishing souls. They are Christians who sacrificially spend valuable life and time engaging in purposeful, spiritual battle in the interest of God's people and his kingdom. These are regular believers who are ever ready to abandon their personal problems to wrestle until the needs of other people are met. They are the ones who stand in the gap, crying before God day and night, until there is solution to the situation in question.

Without intercessors, people and society will come to sudden destruction. The devil is the worst adversary of mankind, and will not hesitate to do great harm if he and his agents are not resisted through prayer.

"Be sober, be vigilant; because your adversary the devil, as a roaring lion, walketh about, seeking whom he may devour" (1 Peter 5:8)

During times of anguish, loneliness, sickness, despair, disappointment or sorrow, the Christian can get distracted by these challenges and become weak in prayer. This is why and where intercessory prayers are very important, as they provide the necessary shield that keeps the menacing devil away.

Intercessors are dear to the heart of God. He needs them, uses them, and not only rewards them, but their prayer of intercession.

7). Prayer of Praise. (Psalms 96: 1-11; 149: 1-9).

The secret of easy access into the presence of God lies in praise. Praise is the key that opens the heart of God. Praise does not only open the curtains of heaven for unhindered thoroughfare, but along with thanksgiving provides that rare unique insight into the activities in the courts of God.

> ***"Enter into his gates with thanksgiving, and into his courts with praise: be thankful unto him, and praise his name". (Psalms 100: 4).***

Praise honors God. A cheerful session of praise before the almighty unlocks the doors of immeasurable favor in the areas of spiritual strength, visions, revelations, and power that enables the Christian to minister in the gifts of the Holy Spirit.

The name, Judah, means praise. Each time the tribe of Judah led the children of Israel in battle, the nation won astounding victory. The walls of Jericho collapsed on account of praise (Joshua 6:1--20). And when Apostle Paul and his traveling companion Silas, were imprisoned in Philippi for preaching the gospel, they prayed and sang praises until the Holy Spirit came to their rescue (Acts 16:i6—26).

Joyful praise draws the attention of the heathen to righteous worship, causing them to admit the goodness of God and to glorify his holy name (Psalms 126:1-2). When God is praised from a joy full heart, the earth bursts forth with abundant harvest, in addition to experiencing an over flow of divine blessings.

> ***"Let the people praise thee, O God; let the people praise thee. Then shall the earth yield***

> ***her increase, and God, even our God, shall bless us" (Psalms 67:6).***

There is indeed great power in praise. Praise and worship are the only elements of prayer that will continue in heaven after the rapture. That is the reason every Christian who hopes to make the rapture at the second coming of Christ, and be part of the marriage super of the lamb, must begin to grow in the art of praise.

Though the art of praise is a sacred act, it can ill afford to ignore the inclusion of instruments, adoption of joyful noise and dance that distinguished King David's prayer style.

> ***"O clap your hands, all people: shout unto God with the voice of triumph" (Psalms 47:1 KJV).***

> ***"Make a joyful noise unto God, all ye lands: Sing forth the honor of his name: make his praise glorious" (Psalms 66: 1)***

> ***"Clap your, all peoples! Shout to God with loud songs of joy!" (Psalms 47:1 ESV).***

> ***"Let Israel rejoice in him that that made him: let the children of Zion be joyful in their King. Let them praise his name in dance: let them sing praises unto him with the timbrel and harp. For the Lord taketh pleasure in his people: he will beautify the meek with salvation. Let the saints be joyful in glory: let them sing aloud upon their beds. Let the high praises of God be***

> ***in their mouth, and a two edged sword in their hand;" (Psalms 149: 3-6).***

Praise goes well with "holy wildness". It worked for David, it will work you.

8). Prayer of Faith. (James 5:15).

Nothing pleases God more than the prayer of faith. This is because faith is taking him at his word. It is the Christian's confidence in God that inspires that total submission to God and his word without doubt.

Faith is the conviction in the natural man that removes every veil of mistrust in his conscience, thus helping in his acceptance of God as a supernatural being that exists, and who is reliable to be trusted. It is the basis of the Christian belief which leads him to trust that God is what he says he is: "The Eternal God", "The Supreme One", "Almighty", "All knowing", "Ever present God", and "The creator of all things". It is this absolute reliance on the worthiness of God by a Christian that drives the engine of prayer.

Faith is a very critical component of prayer. It is as the Christian applies faith in his communication with heaven that he attracts the attention of God. Faith is completely trusting God. It is that absolute confidence in a person that enables him to venture out and begin to act as if the things believed in God for, even when they have not manifested in reality, are already there in existence.

Living-faith goes beyond the perception of what can be seen, touched, felt, or heard. This absolute repose of confidence is very necessary in getting a person's prayer answered. It is so vital that an un-serious believer who prays, taking God at his word can get his petition answered, whereas a practicing Christian who fails to apply his faith may not get any reasonable response (Matthew 8: 5-7).

However, God will answer every prayer irrespective of the level of faith, but it must be there, or you did not pray. While some outstanding preachers like Charles Spurgeon believe that***: "Little faith will bring your soul to heaven, but great faith will bring heaven to you"***, Jesus Christ the greatest teacher of all time taught his disciples that faith is not about size, but the confidence that "he who has promised, is also able to fulfill his word". Thus, it is the absence of unbelief, and not the size of faith that is required to move "mountains". And Jesus said unto them:

> ***"Because of your unbelief, for verily I say unto you, if you have faith as a grain of mustard seed, ye shall say unto this mountain, 'Remove hence to yonder place,' and it shall remove. And nothing shall be impossible unto you". (Matthew 17: 20)***

Faith is the factor that separates real prayer warriors from the mere good ones. It is a concept that translates a person's genuine pursuits into reality. Faith believes before it receives, serving as the tangible evidence for the things perceived with the eye of the spirit-man that are yet to be seen in the natural realm, the title deed of the things acquired in the supernatural realm waiting for possession in the natural plane. It is the hope for the material substances which are in expectation, but are yet to manifest. Faith keeps hope alive. It is the oil that keeps its flame burning.

Prayer that is not backed by faith is mere religious mockery that makes the whole concept of seeking the face of God a wasted effort; it is as well, an irrelevant spiritual exercise. When you pray, have faith in God.

9). Groaning Prayer. (John11: 1-33).

Under normal circumstances, not many people will have the need to groan. This is because groaning in the real sense of the word requires the expression of deep emotion caused by pain, grief, or anguish. The same also holds for groaning in prayer. Unfortunately, while many people easily groan for natural reasons, only a few can turn the anguish, bitterness, and grief of their pain into a useful weapon on the altar of prayer.

Available bible accounts show that only few people are on record for having engaged in the art of "groaning prayer". One example was Jesus at the graveside of Lazarus (John 11:33), and a second time was the same Jesus as he prayed at the Mount of Olives before the arrest that led to his trial and crucifixion (Luke 22: 39-44). Finally, the last agonizing cry of Jesus before he gave up the ghost at Golgotha is another example of the groaning prayer.

Groaning in prayer is one of the highest levels of spiritual dialogue with God. It is indicative of deep agony from a person in right standing to the One who is able to deliver him; it comprises the deep moaning's of a seemingly helpless person at the feet of the **"help of the helpless"** whose name is **Jehovah**. And sure enough, God never abandons the Christian who comes to him groaning in prayer. He always shows up in the storm(s) of anyone whose ways are right with him as the psalmist confirms in this scripture:

> ***"Offer unto God thanksgiving; and pay thy vows unto the most High: And call upon me in the day of trouble: I will deliver thee, and thou shall glorify me". (Psalms 50: 14-15).***

With God, there is the assurance of intervention when a believer who is in right standing, groans before heaven.

10). Travailing Prayer.

To travail is to labor, work hard, toil, or to agonize. It describes some form of wrestling in a situation that can only be achieved with increased effort. It symbolizes serious exercise, and can also imply pains-taking activity, or arduous work.

The method Prophet Elijah adopted on Mount Carmel is the best illustration of the travailing prayer (1 kings18: 42). For three and a half years, this man of God through the dint of prayer had locked up the firmament above Judah. By his command and at the word of God, there was neither rain nor dew. A severe drought and famine ensued, animals began to die, and the harsh reality of Elijah's proclamation spread all over the kingdom, even into the palace of King Ahab. The prophet was declared a wanted person by the king. Then as the king's servants were searching for him, the prophet suddenly re-appears on the scene; but this time with a mandate from God to counter the "no rain decree".

A little while before on mountain Carmel, Elijah had built a make-shift altar, and at the hour of prayer offered up his sacrifice to the living God, which was consumed by liquid fire from heaven. This singular act which gave Elijah victory over the prophets of Baal and the groves, proved to be the surest sign of divine endorsement of him before the people of Israel

(1Kings 18:21-24), leading to the arrest and destruction of all eight hundred and fifty of these false prophets who ate at the table of Jezebel (1 kings 18: 16-40).

At the end of this unique contest, Prophet Elijah went into a session of travailing prayer the purpose of which was to reverse his earlier decree, and open up the heavens for rain.

> ***"And Elijah said unto Ahab, Get thee up, eat and drink; for there is a sound of abundance of rain. Also Ahab went to eat and to drink. And Elijah went up to the top of Carmel; and he cast down himself down upon the earth, and put his face between his knees" (1 kings 18:41-42).***

Elijah's position in this prayer session was both uncommon and unusual, clearly illustrating how tough situations can be dealt with by applying tougher approach. The Prophet had earlier decreed there would be no rain or dew. Now, he needed to cancel the command, a procedure that called for harder work. He did work hard at it, and eventually prevailed.

This is a tasking position to take in prayer, but is the recommended approach when situations become hard to handle in life.

11). Prayer of Petition (Matthew 7: 7).

The principle involved in the prayer of petition is one of action. I call it the ASK procedure. That is:

A—For ask.
S—For seek.
K—For knock.

But whether you choose to ask, seek, or knock, it must be done in faith and according to the will of God for you.

God is always ready for discussion, anxiously waiting to hear from the petitioner. And even when he is able to give more than anyone can ask or think, he still demands that Christian initiate the request. It is his good pleasure to respond to the demands that are brought before him which are in line with his will for the petitioner. So, the onus to initiate the process lies with that believer to whom all options are available, whether to ask, seek, knock or apply these factors in any combination. While there is ample flexibility on the platform of prayer, it is important to apply appropriate options that are most relevant to an individual's need. And as long as the motive is right and in the will of God, such petitions will not only attract audience in the presence of God, but also receive the commensurate response.

12). Prayer to Bind, and to Loose.

The Christian by his position in Christ has been empowered with the authority to address challenging situations; to bind, and to loose ***"whatsoever things"*** (Matthew 16:19). Therefore, when his prayer is backed by God's word, it ought to be respected by every element on earth as well as the authorities in heaven. This is because God stands behind his word to perform or perfect it.

> ***"Verily I say unto you, whatsoever ye shall bind on earth shall be bound in heaven: and whatsoever ye shall loose on earth shall be loosed in heaven" (Matthew 18: 18).***

God has the final say in any situation. He is the one who speaks and it comes to pass. And now, he has elevated Christians, through Christ, to a position from where their commands will have the desired effect because they are backed by his authority in heaven.

13). Holy, violent Prayer. (Matthew 12: 11).

In spiritual warfare, every difficult situation requires corresponding holy, but aggressive action. Some challenges will not just surrender until they come under heavy spiritual artillery. They will not give up until the prayer warrior enlists the backing of heaven. It is in such circumstances that the holy, violent prayer method comes in handy. It is a very useful arsenal in spiritual warfare. The Christian is not to be overtly naïve to think that the devil can be pampered by gentility, negotiation, or coward submission. The adversary is a shameless, lawless warrior who fights without rules. And he does not require any aggravation to start a battle. That is the reason the Christian must be prepared all the time, ever ready to respond with holy, violent aggression against him, his agents, and their strategies. No one ever succeeded against the devil by confronting him with kid gloves. Jesus Christ tacitly commended the holy, violent method of prayer when he said:

> ***"And from the days of John the Baptist until now, the kingdom of Heaven suffereth violence, and the violent take it by force"*** (Matthew 11: 12).

Prophet Elijah's action on Mount Carmel was a classic exercise of authority through holy, violent display in prayer. It resulted in the disgrace and destruction of false prophets, and their tactics (1 kings 18: 20-40).

Every prayer warrior is a soldier of the Lord. Soldiers are bold, fearless, fierce in action, and violent in battle. Jesus always commanded evil spirits with authority. When he cast out a legion of demons, he authoritatively ordered them into a herd of swine, and commanded the swine to run into the river, where they all drowned. ***"This honor, have all his saints"*** (Psalms 149:9).

No saint should ever engage in negotiations with the devil or attempt to pamper his demons. The only instruction they honor is the command of holy violence forceful issued in the name of Jesus by a faithful believer who knows his kingdom right.

14). Warfare Prayer.

Most battles people will face in life will not be physical in nature. This is because these battles originate from the spirit realm. A person's life will end in disaster if natural, conventional weapons of battle are employed to confront such issues.

Warfare prayers are for those who are determined to address stubborn problems, and dismantle the evil powerhouse behind them. So while this method of prayer is the preserve of all believers, those experiencing cycle of spiritual afflictions, and unexplainable physical challenges will find it more useful.

To adequately address their troubling issues, this category of persons must employ this wise strategy of battle.

> ***"For though we walk in the flesh, we do not war according to the flesh. For the weapons of our warfare are not carnal, but mighty through***

> ***God for the pulling down of strongholds, casting down imaginations and every high thing that exalted itself against the knowledge of God, and bringing into captivity every thought to the obedience of Christ" (2 Corinthians 10: 3-5).***

A few of the problems that may require warfare strategies include:

- Eating in the dream.
- Flying like a bird in the dream.
- Experiencing regular dream, sexual encounters with identifiable or unknown persons, popularly known as wet dreams.
- When chased by animals like snakes, dogs, lions, cows, in the dream.
- Getting married or being wedded in the dream.
- Walking about naked in the dream.
- Walking bare-footed in the dream.
- Bearing children in the dream, when you cannot conceive in the natural.
- Breast-feeding in the dream.
- Finding it difficult to get married or to stay married.
- Constant challenges in career, or in a person's health.
- Addiction to drugs, tobacco, alcohol, sex, or other inordinate feelings.
- Having suicidal tendencies.
- Hearing evil voices, and seeing strange images.
- Barrenness, inability to conceive, or suffering from constant miscarriages.
- Un-usual cessation of menstrual period.

- Experiencing cycles of un-explainable hardship.
- Those under any curse, spell, or operating under the burden of evil covenant, oath or soul-tie.
- People suffering from any jinx, hex, effect of divination, or enchantment.
- Always in company with deceased relatives or friends, in the dream.
- Loss money or keys in the dream.
- Buying or selling goods in the dream.
- Experiencing blood dreams.
- All time night-mares.
- Attending your own funeral in the dream.
- Living in any bondage or experiencing the power of strongholds.
- Inconclusive examinations and interviews in the dream.
- Hill or mountain climbing in the dream.
- Clothed in rags in the dream.
- Bathing naked, and in public view in the dream.

This list is inconclusive, but gives an insight into certain unbearable situations that call for the application of holy, but aggressive warfare approach in prayer.

Prayer can be combative, not against God, but with him on your side against the enemy or any troublesome situation.

Warfare prayer is best suited for dismantling satanic networks, and confusing evil organized agencies. It is suggested that vigils as well as fasting programs be combined with this method.

You can pray like this:

1). ***River of affliction flowing into my destiny, dry up from your source, in Jesus name.***
2). ***Arrow of bewitchment fired into my life; go back to sender, in Jesus name.***
3). ***Sword of Holy Ghost fire, uproot the tree of poverty growing in my foundation, in Jesus name.***
4). ***With the blood of Jesus, I nullify every dream judgment passed on my life, in Jesus name.***
5). ***Powers using the cover of darkness to attack my destiny be exposed and disgraced, in Jesus name.***
6). ***Holy Ghost fire, destroy the condolence register opened for my life, in Jesus name.***

15). Decreeing Prayer.

A decree is an order having the force of the law. From the perspective of spiritual warfare, it is an ordinance backed by the authority of God's word. It is a divine process approved by God for the purpose of condemning wicked acts and bringing evil forces under control.

Although there can be silent prayer if the situation demands, the general principle behind the concept of prayer lies in the verbalization of the word of God. It involves speaking to God, and hearing from him. Thus, the medium of expression most suitable for divine decrees is the tried, tested, and sure declaration of scripture. It never disappoints.

> ***"So shall my word be that goeth forth out my mouth: it shall not return unto me void, but it shall accomplish that which I please, and***

> ***it shall prosper in the thing whereto I sent it" (Isaiah 55:11).***

So, as long as the decree, the command, or the declaration is in line with the word of God, it shall be established.

> ***"Thou shalt also decree a thing, and it shall be established unto thee; and the light shall shine upon thy ways" (Job 22: 28).***

Preliminary to the epic combat between David and Goliath the Philistine, we encounter an incredible exchange of decrees in prayer. Goliath's obvious intention was to kill any leader Israel would pitch against him, give his flesh to the birds of the air, and take the nation of Israel as slaves. And he did not hide this, because for forty days and nights he had been on that battle field, openly declaring his intention. However, when David appeared on the scene, he countered Goliath's decree by the authority of a higher power. At the end of the day, David's decree which was backed by heaven overcame the demon, inspired boasts made by Goliath. Thus, the word of God in David's mouth, spoken over Goliath's life, eventually prevailed.

16). Prayer of Agreement. (Matthew 18: 19).

A three way cord is stronger than one. That is why the power of agreement prayer cannot be underestimated. The joint prayer of two or more spirit-filled believers based on the word of God surely attracts the favor of heaven. According to the scripture:

> ***"One man of you shall chase a thousand, for the Lord your God, he it is that fighteth for you, as he has promised you" (Joshua 23:10).***

This is the promise of God for the praying Christian.

However, when two or more of such believers join themselves on any issue, they are able to shunt power between themselves and to inflict greater damage to the enemy and his agents.

> ***"And five of you shall chase an hundred, and a hundred of you shall put ten thousand to flight: and your enemies shall fall before you by the sword" (Leviticus 26:8).***

This is the power of agreement prayer.

17). Prophetic Prayer.

The prophetic type of prayer has often been misunderstood to represent the prayers specifically reserved for people who operate in the office of the prophet. While this is just a piece of the model, the whole truth is that every believer has the right to pray in the prophetic manner.

In the prophetic manner of prayer, a believer asserts divine authority under the anointing of the Holy Spirit who enables the Christian so inspired to fearlessly declare as well as boldly pronounce divine promises enshrined in the word of God upon himself or others.

The prayer warrior that chooses to engage in prophetic style of prayer will confidently make positive declarations over a person, people, land, situation or thing, like Jesus often did. They take authority in the word of God and make holy declarations over anything and everything, living and non-living things alike (Numbers 20:8--11).

This requires a lot of humility, spiritual guts, good knowledge of the scriptures, right standing with God, and un-shakable faith (Luke 15: 5-6). It can be very effective, and attracts instant results.

Scriptural examples of prophetic prayers include:

1). David's response to Goliath (1Samuel 17:37, 45-46).
2). Elijah's command before King Ahab.

> ***"And Elijah the Tishbite, who was of the inhabitants of Gilead, said unto Ahab, As the Lord God of Israel liveth, before whom I stand, there shall not be dew nor rain these years, but according to my word" (1 Kings7:1).***

This is also the kind of prayer that God, through Moses, instructed Aaron the high priest to always declare over the children of Israel. Aaron was not a prophet, but God required him to pray in this prophetic manner over the children of Israel:

> ***"The Lord bless thee, and keep thee: The Lord make his face shine upon thee, and be gracious unto you: The Lord lift up his countenance upon thee, and give thee peace" (Numbers 6:22-26).***

You too can pray in the same way, especially if you have a deep knowledge of God's word, are bold in the application of it, and confident that the God whose word you have spoken is faithful to stand by it.

18). Meditation.

This is a very effective medium of prayer, but one of the least practiced. The reason is probably due to the righteous discipline it requires, the fear of venturing beyond the confines of sound biblical truths into the mysticism of Far-Eastern religions, or total ignorance of the rich benefits of this concept.

Meditation is an attitude of prayer that involves sacred reflection upon divine issues. It is a solemn attitude in worship that deeply dwells on the word of God, remembering what is says, and committing to live by its requirements. A biblical recommendation of this medium is found in the book of Joshua.

> ***"This book of the law shall not depart out of thy mouth; but thou shalt meditate therein day and night, that thou mayest observe to do according to all that is written therein: for then thou shalt make thy way prosperous, and thou shalt have good success" (Joshua 1:8).***

The practice of meditation in prayer helps the soul to stay focused on righteous matters (Philippian's 4:8). It also serves as a veritable tool of discipline in training for a right relationship with God.

> ***"Set your affection on things above, not on things on the earth" (Colossians 3:2).***

Bible endorsed reflections of this nature are those that focus on serious considerations of the attributes of God, the deeper knowledge of his truth, as well as the sound application of experiences gained from such exercises for proper spiritual growth.

Meditating on the word and person of God is not only a means of inviting Christ into a life, but by implication is a submission to the fatherhood of God of the bible.

This habit if practiced regularly can become a reflex to the advantage of the praying saint

PRAYER POINTS.

1). My father, I acknowledge my sins before you, forgive me, in Jesus name.
2). O Lord, save me from the guilt of ancestral iniquity, in Jesus name.
3). Holy Ghost fire, deliver me from the bondage of evil heritage, in Jesus name.
4). Blood of Jesus, wash away my sins, in Jesus name.
5). My prayer shall open the windows of heaven in my favor, in Jesus name.
6). Thank you Lord, for rescuing me when I cried unto, in Jesus name.
7). Grace and mercy of God incubate me, in Jesus name.
8). By the word of God, I decree prosperity into my life, in Jesus name.
9). O Lord, open my eyes that I may see what you have set before me, in Jesus name.
10). By the authority in name of Jesus, I receive power to crush the serpent of poverty, and scorpion of infirmity, in Jesus name.

Chapter 4

CONDITIONS OF PRAYER.

There are un-avoidable principles for private or corporate prayer that make access into the presence of God very easy. These are conditions that must not be missing from any meaningful prayer checklist. What you will find below are not in way exhaustive, but are good steps in the right direction.

1).You must be born again.

The new –birth experience is important to that person who desires to achieve reasonable results in prayer. You must be born again or already have Christ as your personal Lord and Savior. The reason here is because Christ is the only channel through which anyone can connect with God.

"I am the way, the truth, and the life: no man cometh unto the Father, but by me" (John 14:6).

No one can go directly to God without passing through Jesus.

The new-birth experience involves the simple process of surrendering a person's old ways to Jesus, and accepting the new life that he offers. This is referred to as being born again, and requires the simple steps of confessing the Lordship of the Savior in recognition of his birth, ministry, death, and resurrection.

> ***"That if thou shalt confess with thy mouth the Lord Jesus, and shall believe in thine heart that God raised him from the dead, thou shalt be saved"* (Romans 10:9).**

This is the first major step to attracting God's attention in the arena of prayer. You must be born again.

2). Make your way right with God.

God demands spiritual, moral, and social accountability from man. As a result, a good measure of holy conduct and godliness which though not equal, but is comparable in an equivalent manner on the earth plane to the level that obtains in the heavenly realm, should accompany every genuine prayer effort. Sin separates man from God, and hinders him from doing God's will. So it is by the honest acts of repentance and renunciation of sin that anyone can be ready to pray:

> ***"Thy will be done on earth, as it is in heaven" (Matthew 6: 10).***

However, while no earthly being can attain to God's state of righteousness, yet God demands strict human commitment to those spiritual values that characterize his likeness in man, which also shape the moral structure of human society and signify man's readiness for fellowship.

Although God perceives every life through the mirror of Christ's righteousness, the Christian must strive to always live by the inherent virtues of God in him. While this may seem difficult to achieve, it can be realized through complete submission of such life to Christ in whom all believers live and have their being.

It is only through such surrender that the penitent sinner can make his way right, and be reconciled with God.

"For God has not called us unto uncleanness, but unto holiness" (1 Thessalonians 4: 7)

Righteousness is a sign of godliness. God is Holy, spiritually perfect in nature and in all his ways. He will not tolerate sin, and expects all who deal with him to do so in moral purity. By the sacrifice of Jesus, the Christian has been redeemed. They thus become Christ's just as he is theirs; his holiness living inside of them.

So God delights in the steps the believer takes to live right with him. The moment a person gets born again, he or she becomes called to a life in holiness and righteousness that is no less in standard than God expects for all his children. A righteous believer does not only please God, but enjoys the benefits of righteousness which include the peace of the Lord, and joy of the Holy Ghost.

3). Pray with faith.

Faith in prayer is a factor that is inevitable. They work together, are inseparable, and cannot do without one another. The concept of prayer implies a life of faith. It suggests a belief and absolute confidence in someone you have never seen, but whom you trust will do what he says he has promised. The identity of every genuine Christian is their unwavering confidence in God. So all the believer's prayers, though based on the word of God, must be rested on absolute confidence that God is able to bring to pass, what he says he can do.

Prayer without faith will not prevail; neither will faith with no prayer yield any tangible results.

However, when the two are combined, challenges are subdued, problems bow, and mountains are removed.

> ***"But without faith it is impossible to please him: for he that cometh to God must believe that he is, and that he is a rewarder of them that diligently seek him". (Hebrews 11:6)***

So, faith is that inevitable factor that separates a serious Christian from the ordinary believer. Faith is the identity of the prayer warriors that differentiates them from "worriers" who say they believe, but put their trust in other gods, idols of man, the occult, witchcraft, science, or philosophy.

Faith is the marriage between confidence in God and the believer's absolute surrender at the feet of Jesus. It is that distinctive factor that pre-qualifies a petitioner's challenges for divine attention, enhancing the chances of favorable answers to questions brought before the court of heaven.

4). Good knowledge, and timely application of the word of God.

The bible is undoubtedly the greatest book in any form, in circulation. However, it will not be held in such high esteem if its greatness lay only in the number in circulation.

It is indeed a noble pursuit to search it out, not just with passivity, but with a curiosity to understand it. A good knowledge, regular and timely application of the word of God serves as solid ground to stand on in times of temptation and against the devil.

On three instances Jesus was tempted by Satan in the wilderness, he overcame the devil by applying appropriate scriptures (Matthew 4:1—11).

> ***"And when the tempter came to him, he said, If thou be the Son of God, command that these stones be made bread (Matthew 4:3).***

> ***But he answered and said, It is written, Man shall not live by bread alone, but by every word that proceedeth out of the mouth of God"(Matthew 4:4; Deuteronomy 8:3).***

> ***"Then the devil taketh him up into the holy city, and setteth him on a pinnacle of the temple, And said unto him, If thou be the Son of God, cast thyself down: for it is written, He shall give his angels charge concerning thee: and in their hands they shall bear thee up, lest at any time thou dash thy foot against a stone" (Matthew 4:5—6; Psalms 91:11—12).***

> ***"Jesus said unto him, It is written again, Thou shall not tempt the Lord thy God" (Matthew 4:7; Deuteronomy 6:16).***
>
> ***"Again, the devil taketh him up into an exceeding high mountain, and showeth him all the kingdoms of the world, and the glory of them; And saith unto him, All these things will I give thee, if thou wilt fall down and worship me (Matthew4:8—9)***
>
> ***Then saith Jesus unto him, Get thee hence, Satan: for it is written, Thou shalt worship the Lord thy God, and him only shalt thou serve" (Matthew 4:10; Deuteronomy 6:13).***

When you pray, apply scriptures that are relevant to the situation you want to address. The word of God is living and active. As it is spoken with faith, it activates a response from heaven causing what you commanded to be established (Psalms 119:89).

That is why it is important not just to know the word of God, but when and how to apply it. The rich knowledge of the word of God, its timely and appropriate application will keep sin away, help one in ministry, as well as strengthen the Christian in time of trouble (Clossians3:16).

5). Seek the help of the Holy Spirit.

Be a friend of the Holy Spirit. He is the third person of God and the one who gives strength for prayer. Many believers relegate the divine Holy Spirit to the background. They never think about him or remember him in their regular interaction with heaven. Some scarcely appreciate that the Holy Spirit is a divine person like God and Jesus Christ. But he is indeed an indispensable player in the team of the Holy trinity. The Holy Spirit is such a great help and partner in matters of divine courtship that no prayer warrior worthy of his claim can afford to neglect him.

Jesus relied on him tremendously during his earthly ministry, and promised believers the Gift of this Spirit as his replacement.

Jesus said:

> ***"If you love me, keep my commandments, And I will pray the father, and he shall give you another comforter, that he may abide with you forever; Even the Spirit of truth; whom the world cannot receive, because it seeth him not, neither knoweth him: but ye know him; for he dwelleth with you, and shall be in you" (John 14:15-17).***

Every prayer warrior needs the help of the Holy Spirit. He is equal partner with God responsible for reviving our weak bodies with the spiritual energy necessary to overcome the weariness often experienced at the altar of prayer.

> ***"Likewise the Spirit also helpeth our infirmities: for we know not what we should pray for as we ought: but the Spirit itself maketh intercession for us with groanings which cannot be uttered"*** (Romans 8:26).

The Holy Spirit is too valuable for any prayer warrior to ignore. That is why it is necessary to court his favor if you must have enduring relationship with God.

6). Pray in the name of Jesus.

The need for a believer to pray in the name of JESUS can never be over emphasized. The name of Jesus is the believer's trump card. You risk all in prayer when you refuse to apply it, or do not pray in the authority of his name. It is a name that is honored in heaven, and that is feared as well in hell.

> ***"The God of Abraham, and of Isaac, and of Jacob, the God of our fathers, hath glorified his Son Jesus; whom you delivered up, and denied him in the presence of Pilate, when he was determined to let him go. But you denied the Holy One and the Just, and desired a murderer to be granted unto you; And killed the prince of life, whom God hath raised from the dead; whereof we are witnesses. And his name through faith in his name hath made this man strong, whom you see and know: yea, the faith which is by him hath given him this perfect soundness in the presence of you all" (Acts 3: 13—16).***

Apostle Peter gave glory to whom glory was due because he knew it was the authority in Jesus' name that made that lame man whole again (Acts 3: 6-7)

The name of Jesus is the password that opens the gates of heaven. After a person has laid there problem at the feet of

God in the name of Jesus, no mountain can be high to climb, no river so deep to swim, no wilderness so wide to cross, or knee too stiff to bend.

7). Be specific.

When you get into the presence of God, do not loiter. Focus on the things that matter. Be specific and concentrate on your main objective.

That was Hannah's strategy. She knew exactly what she desired from God, and went straight for it. It is on biblical record that Samuel was the testimony to Hannah's specific prayer request.

> ***"And she was in bitterness of soul, and prayed unto the Lord, and wept sore. And she vowed a vow, and said, O Lord of hosts, if thou wilt indeed look on the affliction of thine handmaid, and remember me, and not forget thine handmaid, but wilt give unto thine handmaid a man child, then I will give him unto the Lord all the days of his life, and there shall no razor come upon his head" (1 Samuel 1:10-11).***

> ***"And they rose up in the morning early, and worshiped before the Lord, and returned and came to their house in Ramah: and Elkanah knew Hannah his wife: and the Lord remembered her. Wherefore it came to pass, when the time was come about after Hannah had conceived, that she bare a son, and called***

> ***his name Samuel, saying, Because I have asked him of the Lord" (1Samuel 1:19-20).***

Nehemiah's request to God before approaching King Artaxerxes is another illustration of specificity in prayer. He needed favor before the king, but realizing that God had the control of every king's heart, he evoked the mercy of God while specifically making his request. (Nehemiah 1: 11).

8). Have focus.

Be sure to put aside all distractions when you go to God in prayer. Apostle Paul, in his letter to the believers in Philippi, emphasized the need for focus in this manner:

> ***"Be careful for nothing; but in everything by prayer and supplication with thanksgiving, let your requests be made known unto God" (Philippians 4:6).***

It is difficult not to worry, which explains Apostle Paul's advice to turn any such distractions to God. When you pray, do not allow the cares of life, frustrations, agitations, evil imaginations, or other ungodly emotions to overcome your spirit. These will cause your mind to stray, and take your concentration away from the source of your help. Avoid them, focus on the immeasurable size of your God, not the magnitude of the problem, and you will see what great things your great God can do.

9). Pray with expectations.

After you have prayed, expect results. Never seek the face of God without looking forward to a tangible response. Even if you only chose to reverence him in worship, praise, or adoration, there is always a blessing in acknowledgment of your worship, waiting to cause a joyful overflow in your life.

The process of waiting after you have prayed may create unnecessary anxiety. However, never allow any apprehensive feeling of uneasiness to steal the joy of a deserved godly anticipation.

God does not delight in your adoration for nothing. He will always reach out to you with some tangible appreciation in return for your confidence and hope.

PRAYER POINTS.

1). Holy Spirit, subdue my anxious moments, in Jesus name.
2). O Lord, open my eyes to see, and strengthen my hands to possess the riches of this land, in Jesus name.
3). By the power of God, I defeat my internal battles, in Jesus name.
4). Holy Ghost fire, move swiftly, and destroy my limitations, in Jesus name.
5). By the authority of heaven, I command the elements to favor me, in Jesus name.
6). I disconnect my destiny from the altar of affliction, in Jesus name.
7). Holy Spirit, turn my weaknesses at the altar of prayer into overcoming-strength, in Jesus name.
8). Holy Spirit, enable me to fulfill my divine purpose, in Jesus name.
9). O Lord, empower me with enough provision to run with my divine vision, in Jesus name.
10). My father, use me to make your kingdom the kind of place you desire it to be, in Jesus name.

Chapter 5

DEFECTS IN PRAYER.

Every time we pray, we want to be sure the exercise was not in vain. We all need that assurance. But the words we speak and the methods we adopt can undermine our chances of victory at the altar of prayer. How a person proceeds in prayer might knock down that sacred ladder that connects the earth with the gates of heaven, putting God out of his reach. This is something we do not want to happen.

Defects in prayer will no doubt introduce un-necessary glitches in the whole exercise, whether or not they were unconsciously intended. But a good understanding of the elements of prayer and the proper application of them can help keep away any flaws. However, until we identify them and be determined to evade their influence on our prayer regimen, they will continue to undermine our efforts.

These prayer erasers are numerous. But by far the most commonly encountered, which must be avoided before, during, and after fellowship with God include:

1). Praying without faith (Mark 11:24).

Faith is a very essential element in prayer. It is so indispensable in the process of divine interaction that it has the potential make or mare a person's prayer.

Apostle Paul's experience, recorded in the epistle to the Hebrews states that:

> ***"Without faith, it is impossible to please God" (Hebrews 11:6).***

Faith is a fundamental element in prayer, the gene around which our thoughts, imaginations, and all emotional expressions are framed.

> ***"Therefore I say unto you, What things soever you desire, when ye pray, believe that ye receive them, and ye shall have them" (Mark 11:24).***

It is the heart of prayer, the cornerstone of all result oriented interaction with the spiritual realm, and the key that opens the courts of heaven. Whether it is the believing faith required for salvation, faith necessary to appropriate healing, faith for deliverance, or faith to work miracles, you just must have faith in God in order to have audience with him. In fact, faith is such an inevitable factor in the whole concept of prayer that the entire exercise becomes mere religious circus without it.

Faith adds credibility to a person's efforts to reach God. It is the evidence that you know whom you received, believed, and by whose program of salvation you became a son, or daughter of the most high God (John 1:12). Faith not only keeps hope alive, it enables the eyes of the natural man to see into the supernatural realm to perceive the things asked for even before they become real.

Faith brings a person into the realm of the miraculous, the place where God dwells. It is the indispensable opener of the door to his presence. Until that door is open, no one can receive attention in heaven. This is why any prayer exercise that does not have the element of faith will not yield result (Matthew 17:20).

The more intimate a believer gets with God, the more confident they become with handling spiritual and natural issues. Matters that seemed difficult and near impossible in the past begin to look simpler and easier to deal with. Such believers handle difficult challenges with better understanding than those who do not share a faith based intimacy with God.

Faith literally moves mountains. It overcomes all fears, subdues human concerns, and diminishes every cause to worry. It is that steadfast, unshakeable, child- like confidence, that works patience, overpowers trials, and produces wisdom (James 1:3).

Faith is the pillar of prayer. It is the catalyst that quickens its action, and gives it meaning. It is the fire that consumes the sacrifice on the altar, causing a sweet smell to ascend to heaven.

Without faith, you cannot work for God, or walk with him. You make no sense. Your prayer becomes like offering on the altar with no fire to consume it.

2). Prayer of the unrighteous mind (Proverbs 15:29).

An unrighteous mind is one corrupted with sin. He imagines nothing but rebellion, confusion, and mischief. The prayer of an unrighteous person is an affront to God, and a demonic effort to gate crash into God's holy presence. The bible describes such act as an abomination (Proverbs 28:9). The prayer of an unrighteous person is a huge joke that has dire consequences

The Psalmist also says:

> ***"if I regard iniquity in my heart, the Lord will not hear me" (Psalms 66:18).***

Sin separates a person from God, that is why all iniquity must be dealt with, or they will make one ineligible for access into the courts of God (Isaiah 59:2).

The state of the unrighteous soul renders their prayers null and void, except when it is motivated by the need for repentance.

3). Sin.

Sin is any form of thought, word, or deed that rejects the commandment of God, and rebels against his statutes.

Righteousness is godliness. It will endear and connect the human soul to God. But acts of rebellion, gross injustice and wickedness will take a person far away from him.

So, apart from the penitent prayers of confession of sins and repentance, any sinner's effort at reaching God is not only considered spiritual robbery, but a defilement of divine ordained order and disrespect to God.

For the eyes of God, the bible says, are too pure to look on sin (Habakkuk 1:13). King David was a man who experienced the forgiving power of God's love. And he said this about unacknowledged, un-confessed, and un-forsaken sin:

> ***"The foolish shall not stand in thy sight: thou hatest all workers of iniquity" (Psalms 5:5).***

Sin is a great defect. It will disqualify anyone before God.

4). Pride.

The Pharisees prayed with an arrogant attitude which Jesus very much condemned in his time. He called them hypocrites for lack of humility in their dealings with God.

Pride will destroy the bridge of divine fellowship and render the whole exercise of prayer worthless. This is because the individual already presumes in his heart that he is worthy of divine attention, and is qualified for God's favor based on merit, and not by God's grace. According to King Solomon:

> ***"Every one that is proud in the heart is an abomination to the Lord: though hand join in hand, he shall not be unpunished" (Proverbs 16:5).***

Only the foolish can afford the tragic pleasure of arrogance in prayer, for in their mouth is the rod for their own destruction (Proverbs 14:3).

5). Un-forgiveness.

Un-forgiveness is a destructive habit. It is a negative shield that will block a believer's prayer. Thus, the next proper step to take after confession and repentance is the level of forgiveness, as you begin to pardon those you are in conflict with, whether or not you perceive yourself as the aggrieved person, or the other party as the offender.

God's requirement mandates total remission of all grievances, and that the Christian gives up their resentment of others before proceeding to pray. No one can make things right with God without first sorting out their differences with his fellow humans.

God's pattern of forgiveness is based on man's willingness to forgive others. This is clearly stated in the prayer method Jesus taught his disciples:

> ***"And when ye stand praying, forgive, if ye have aught against any: that your Father also which is in heaven may forgive you your trespasses. But if ye do not forgive, neither will your Father which is in heaven forgive your trespasses" (Mark 11:25-26).***

Any form of un-forgiveness will introduce glitches in the efforts to make contact with God.

6). Wrong motive.

Many people pray with the wrong motives in their heart. You may choose to deceive yourself, but you cannot deceive God no matter how much you pretend. Your motive determines whether or not your prayer will receive any fruitful response. According to the Psalmist:

> ***"God is near to all those who call unto him in truth".*** (Psalms 145:18)

As long as your objective is wrong, your request will not even get near the court of heaven as the demand will meet with outright rejection. No one expects to get divine approval for a request that does not glorify God. The apostle James says:

> ***"Ye ask, and receive not, because ye ask amiss, that ye may consume it upon your lusts"*** (James 4:3).

People who ask for divine favors for the wrong reasons will not get a good deal. And if they ever receive any comfort after this type of exercise, it is from the devil, and not from God. That is how disappointing it can be as one prays with the wrong motive.

It is not wrong to pray for one-self and family. However, a selfish prayer protocol that revolves mainly on you, your spouse, and family, can become a serious flaw.

Also, when your prayers focus on matters that are not within divine agenda, matters that do not align with the will of the Holy Spirit, are based on worldly issues that do not affect others positively or add value to God's kingdom, that person will not get any comforting response from God.

7). Lack of Expectation.

Expectation is the hope behind prayer. It justifies the very reason for which the Christian prayed. That element of anticipation after prayer is a further display of confidence in the God to whom the believer looked up to for the realization of his request.

> ***"Therefore I say unto you, What things soever ye desire, when ye pray, believe that ye receive them, and ye shall have them" (Mark 11:24).***

Believing that you have received is the faith element. But the expectation is the spiritual catalyst that works concurrently with faith, to turn what is spiritually hoped for into physical manifestation. It could be a refreshing **YES**, an unpleasant **NO**, or an anxious **WAIT**. But you must expect a result from your effort. If after you reached out to God you did not expect any answer, then you did not really pray. The result you receive may not be what you anticipated, yet it gives you the assurance that God, at least, responded to your prayer.

But praying without expectation is a dangerous religious ritual that ends up creating a void between that Christian and God which can only be attributed to the person's unbelief.

8). Impatience at the altar of prayer.

It is rude and disrespectful to speak to anyone and not wait to hear their response. Communication in any form or manner is a dialogue that involves more than one party. It is the reciprocal giving and receiving of information between individuals through a system common to the parties involved.

In spiritual warfare, it is the verbal exchange between man and God.

Hurrying away from the presence of God, defeats the whole essence of prayer. Only prayer "worriers" do this. To counter this habit, Apostle Paul says:

> ***"Cast not away therefore your confidence, which hath great recompense of reward. For ye have need of patience, that, after ye have done the will of God, ye might receive the promise"*** (Hebrews 10:35-36).

Unfortunately, a lot of people unconsciously hurry away from the presence of God without hearing from him after they have spoken to him. Many people do not hear from God not because he failed to speak, but for the reason that they hurried away even before he responded. Patience is a great Christian virtue. Without it, no believer can gain any tangible blessing from God (Hebrews 6:12). Those who hurry off from the place of prayer risk losing much.

9). **Doubt** (James 1:5-8)

Doubt is a very fatal storm that will destroy even the most genuine objective to seek God's attention. It is a negative emotion that should not be welcome in the place of divine fellowship.

It is a display of no confidence which represents the absence of any trust in God, tragically implying a denial of divine credibility. Doubt emphasizes the feeling of an adverse belief, and a pessimistic perception that leads to no reliance on God's ability to fulfill his promise. It is questioning the certainty of God, or distrusting in his willingness to do what only him can do.

Doubt is synonymous with fear, smacks of a feeling of un-certainty, and clearly represents the absence of hope for a divine response.

To come to the altar of prayer with a feeling of doubt already presumes that you do not believe that God can be trusted to do that which he says he can actually do.

King Solomon's solution to this issue is found in the book of Proverbs.

> ***"Trust in the Lord with all thine heart; and lean not unto thine own understanding" (Proverbs 3:5).***

Any interaction with God that features the element of doubt will surely attract disfavor rather than divine attention. The concept of doubt in its entirety invalidates the very basic principles of divine communication. And more often than not, doubters have a defeatist mentality that welcomes failure instead of success. They tend to accept defeat even before their battle begins, which is a good reason to eliminate this feeling that hinders a person's effort in the process of prayer. It must be avoided before, during, and after all fellowship, communion, and communication with God.

10). Purposeless prayer.

Purpose is the essence of prayer, the primary motive that stirs any desire to encounter God. It is the very reason that inspires the interaction between heaven and earth, the driving force behind a person's conviction to seek divine audience.

Purpose is that underlying factor that generates human desire to make contact with heaven, the fire that kindles our faith and the power behind any real intention to fellowship with God.

A good objective does not only constitute the spark that kindles the fire of prayer, it is the oil that ensures its continuous glow. Without purpose there would be no genuine hunger for God.

However, the goal one sets out to achieve must be right to make the process meaningful. In line with this, Apostle Paul admonished believers in his epistle to the Philippians saying:

> ***"Finally, brethren, whatsoever things are true, whatsoever things are honest, whatsoever things are just, whatsoever things are pure, whatsoever things are lovely, whatsoever things are of a good report, if there be any virtue, and if there be any praise, think on these things"*** (Philippians 4:8).

The motive has to be there, as well as be right. A wrong reason, no matter how compelling will not attract the attention of God.

11). Absentmindedness.

Many honest Christians have experienced this feeling on the altar of prayer. No sooner they began to pray than their minds strayed, led away to some distant place far from the original intention that first inspired their fellowship with God. During such situations, many believers confess to have ended up in such spheres of unrighteous imaginations within their subconscious being that were embarrassing to talk about thereafter.

Absent-mindedness is an adverse factor that will ruin any form of interaction with God. It is a smear on the garment of prayer that should be avoided as it has the power to wreck the beauty of entire exercise.

PRAYER POINTS.

1). O Lord, deliver me from impatience at the altar of prayer, in Jesus name.
2). Holy Spirit, help me to pray for what I need rather than what I want, in Jesus name.
3). My father, let your spirituality always subdue my humanity, in Jesus name.
4). Holy Spirit, purge my mind of evil imaginations, in Jesus name.
5). Holy Spirit, help me to pray with a clean motive, in Jesus name.
6). By the authority of heaven, I uproot any human or satanic barriers to my prayers, in Jesus name.
7). O God arise, and disgrace the wicked powers challenging your authority in my life, in Jesus name.
8). Evil altars responsible for my problems, collapse, in Jesus name.
9). My father, make me to know the exceeding greatness of your power towards me, in Jesus name.
10). Holy Ghost fire, short-circuit the evil communication network eaves-dropping on my prayers, in Jesus name.

Chapter 6

Dangers of Prayerlessness.

1). Powerlessness.

Christians who joke with their prayer lives will undoubtedly become spiritually impotent. Tragic as this may sound, it is the condition in which many find themselves today. Prayerlessness has become the Christian's worst nightmare, and his biggest battle ground of defeat. The devil understands this, which explains the reason he regularly employs this great arsenal against the so called children of light.

The devil can do anything but pray. He is also fully aware of the great power behind the Christian prayer warrior. As a result, he does not want anyone to develop the habit of praying to God or hearing from Him.

Sadly enough, many believers, including prayer warriors, have often strayed onto the slippery slope of prayerlessness, consequently becoming the proverbial "toothless bull dog" that can bark, but cannot bite.

The cage of prayerlessness is the last place any believer would want to be caught inside. This is a dangerous place inside which many Christians, though naturally alive, have been rendered spiritually powerless and dead.

2). Easy prey to the enemy.

Believers who do not develop the prayerful habit will become victims of satanic bewitchment, and easy target for star hunters. The great prophet Isaiah referred to this category of believers as ***"lawful captives of the mighty and the terrible"*** (Isaiah 49:24). When the fire on your prayer altar is dim or completely out, you become easy prey to the devil and his agents.

Problems that destroy people first begin by stealing their prayer life. The moment a person's prayer life is dismantled, that individual becomes a guinea pig in his enemy's satanic laboratory. The devil can do whatever he chooses and whenever with such lives.

Only regular and meaningful prayer regimen will prevent this from happening.

3). A life of anxiety.

Many believers are more inclined to worry than to pray and believe. In this modern generation that has relegated sacred respect for God to the background, concerned Christians need to pray until they have no more need to pray. According to Martin Luther, believers should ***"Pray, and let God worry".***

Those who never pray at all defraud themselves of their heritage in Christ, while those who lace their prayer with ungodly anxiety pray in vain.

Anxiety must not be confused with divine anticipation. For while expectation is the ladder you put in place to assist your ministering angels to get through to you after you have prayed, satanic worry dismantles that ladder. Anxiety does nothing but reveal a lack of no confidence in a person's standing with God.

In this life, there must be someone to trust, that higher supernatural being who can effectively handle challenges beyond your human ability. You either deal with God, or with Satan. Trusting your life with God secures it in the hands of its original maker. But relying on the devil will result in those anxious moments, seasons of uncertainty, and nights of fear that ultimately lead to frustration, disappointment, and destruction.

In Prophet Moses valedictory speech to all Israel, he said:

> ***"I call heaven and earth to record this day against you, that I have set before you life and death, blessing and cursing: therefore choose life that both you and thy seed may live". (Deuteronomy 30: 19).***

So, you rather choose God and live than be consumed with ceaseless worry for the unknown because you bet with the devil.

4). A restless life.

A life burdened by stress, bowed by despair, and overcome by disappointment will show weariness at the altar of prayer. Rather than bring comfort, such feelings lead to further disillusionment, confusion, and restlessness.

However, the weary soul that surrenders his boredom to Christ will find hope and rest in God.

> ***"Come unto me, all ye that labour and are heavy laden, and I will give you rest (Matthew 11:28).***

A life that does not pray, or which operates from a weak prayer altar is a life in jeopardy. Such people are often restless from being unable to resolve even the simplest challenges. As a result, they become desperate in life, qualifying as prospective recruits in the camp of the devil.

The devil loves Christians who do not appreciate the benefits and power of prayer, and would do anything possible to keep a believer from engaging the holy God in conversation, especially by preventing such people from praying in the name of Jesus.

Prayerlessness puts a person on an endless downward spiral. It erodes all hope, and locks its victim out of the doors of divine goodness from where help can be sought when the situation demands. It imposes limitations on God, making him unable come to the person's recue in the time of dire need. It is consciously electing to walk the wide way of worry, anxiety, frustration, disappointment, and destruction, rather than follow the narrow, but sure paths of righteousness, peace, and joy in the Holy Ghost that lead to the presence of God

PRAYER POINTS.

1). Power for total surrender, envelop my life, in Jesus name.
2). O Lord, lead me in thy righteous paths, in Jesus name.
3). Holy Spirit, make your way plain before my eyes, in Jesus name.
4). Spirit of God, strengthen me in the time of prayer, in Jesus name.
5). Holy Spirit, lead me to pray according to the mind of God, in Jesus name.
6). Holy Ghost fire, ignite my altar of prayer, in Jesus name.
7). Holy Spirit, give me a patient soul, a discerning mind, and an obedient spirit in my prayer life, in Jesus name.
8). Finger of God, up-root any sin that will hinder the victory of prayer in my life, in Jesus name.
9). Holy Spirit, help me to develop the faith that destroys doubt, in Jesus name.
10). O Lord, wake me up from spiritual slumber, in Jesus name.

Chapter 7

BENEFITS OF PRAYER.

Result oriented prayer addicts are blessed children of God. These are the overcomers and Christians who became victors in battle because they never gave up on prayer. They experience outstanding successes in areas where prayer midgets will not dare. They are the Elijah's of this generation who know the God before whom they stand (1 Kinds 17:1).

That Christian who finds the mystery of prayer secures for himself the only sure way to all-round prosperity that the spiritually naïve believer can never find. There is without doubt a secret to total prosperity which is found in ceaseless prayer of faith to a holy and compassionate God. In this secret lies the key to chamber of divine benefits.

Some of these benefits include:

1). A life of healing and good health.

One of the numerous titles by which God revealed himself is: ***"The Lord that heals" (Exodus 15:26).*** God indeed is the one that heals. Prayer is a clear evidence of human allegiance to God, and a sign of covenant relationship with him. God's promise to his covenant children is to save them from sickness and diseases. That is why many of God's laws and statutes were framed to keep sickness away from his obedient children.

So as a Christian pleads for strength in prayer to resist the temptation of fornication or adultery, he is praying to be in good health. Those who fall prey to these sexual sins not only defile their bodies, but also expose themselves to the dangers of promiscuity.

Hence, those who go to God in prayer with a spirit, soul, and body fully compliant to his commandment receive the divine protective shield that ensures healing and good health.

Moreover, when a prayer warrior evokes the blood of Jesus or prays by the authority in the name of Jesus, he creates a favorable atmosphere for healing. Testimonies of restored health abound from people who trusted in God for healing and prayed over an infirmity. The gift to heal, and to remain in a state of good health is a privilege reserved for God's obedient children.

It is the Holy Spirit that imparts this gift. Yet it cannot be released except by engaging in intimate friendship and constant fellowship with the third person of the trinity. This is what effectual, fervent prayer can achieve.

2). Total deliverance.

Prayer is the power behind deliverance. The divine invitation to set captives free is a commandment to all

Christians. However, due to the very complex nature of this ministry, God empowers only those servants he can trust with power to execute this assignment (Psalms 149:1—9).

These are called deliverance ministers. They are bold, fearless, trusted, honest, and righteous prayerful Christians who have the special call of God for the task of setting captives free. It is such Christians that God uses to bring spiritual and physical deliverance to person(s) or people in his kingdom that are living in any kind of bondage. The "mad man of Gadarene" who Jesus ministered to, regained his right mind and began enjoying total freedom from demonic possession, because Jesus prayed for him (Mark 5:1—15).

Moses excelled in this gift, Prophet Elijah operated greatly in it, and the Lord Jesus Christ was the greatest of all deliverance ministers.

He not only delivered entire humanity from captivity through his selfless sacrifice on the cross, he set those in satanic bondage free from all forms of demonic oppression, possession, and obsession, during his earthly ministry. Demons trembled at Jesus appearance, and he never hesitated from casting them out of their victims, ensuring that such people regained their liberty, the right mindset, and good state of health.

3). Ability to hear from God.

Prayer is asking questions, and expecting answers. God responds to your enquiries either while still praying, or in some silent period thereafter. In such serene atmosphere, God responds to the faith- backed requests that have been presented before him by providing privileged information from his throne. (Daniel 2:1-49).

As a person grows in sacred fellowship with the Almighty, he begins to experience supernatural encounters that reveal what others cannot see, hear, or feel. These are what the bible refers to as mysteries, or the "secret things" that belong to the Lord.

> ***"The secret things belong unto the Lord, but those things which are revealed belong unto us and to our children forever, that we may do all the words of this law" (Deuteronomy 29:29).***

God reveals valuable mysteries to faithful Christians who are committed, and are readily available to use such knowledge to honor God and serve humanity.

4). Reigning in kingdom peace and joy.

The surest place for basking in the fullness of divine prosperity is in the presence of God. Some of the graces available here, among numerous others, include kingdom peace and joy (Philippians 4:6). So, through constant communication with God, a person can gain unhindered insight or access into heaven to possess unsearchable riches that are beyond ordinary human understanding and the reach of those who do not enjoy such covenant relationship.

> ***"And the peace of God, which passeth all understanding, shall keep your hearts and minds through Christ Jesus" (Philippians 4:7).***

5). Power for clear visions. (Proverbs 29:18)

A prayerful person can be sure of regularly enjoying wonderful rewards such as destiny directing dreams, clear visions, and deep spiritual revelations. Praying to God prepares the atmosphere for divine opportunities, and exposes such Christians to privileges reserved only for believers who stay in the presence of God all the time.

Abraham was such a person. He was a man who knew the importance of prayer altars, built them wherever he went, and prayed selflessly offering sacrifices there to the living God. As a result, God blessed him with visions, which revealed future events about his destiny to which we are witnesses today (Genesis 15:1-6).

In one out of the numerous divine encounters Abraham had, God used the picture of the innumerable stars of heaven to give him an idea of the uncountable number of biological descendants that would survive him. Ironically at this late stage of life he and Sarah his wife had not had any child between them. Yet, Abraham faithfully believed this promise, holding God to his word in prayer until the birth of Isaac, by his wife Sarah (Genesis 18: 17-19).

The sacred experience Abraham had in that session of fellowship with God is generally described as a vision. Visions come from God. They represent the momentary opening of the will of God to the carnal man for instruction, assignment or knowledge. Through such experience a person can clearly see and understand the path to follow in life (Proverbs 25:12), and receive privileged guidance from heaven (Proverbs 32:18).

6). Prayer edifies the body.

Prayer helps to edify the body, and to renew the spirit.. One of the roles of the Holy Spirit is to give help in time of prayer. To comfort, console, and encourage the saint's effort. There is an invitation to the Holy Spirit as a person prepares or begins to pray. And the subsequent intervention by the Holy Spirit is usually perceived as divine endorsement of that individual's or group's effort, which comes along with benefits.

Through prayer the carnal man receives strength to revive his spirit, renew his soul, and spiritual nourishment to rebuild his body in areas where stress, anguish, frustration, depression, disappointment or sickness may have taken their toll.

> ***"Likewise the Spirit also helpeth our infirmities, for we know not what we should pray for as we ought: but the Spirit itself maketh intercession for us with groaning's, which cannot be uttered. And he that searcheth the hearts knoweth what is the mind of the Spirit, because he maketh intercession for the saints according to the will of God".***
> (Romans 8: 26-27)

So, whenever the believer begins to engage God in prayer, the Holy Spirit comes in to give him support.

7). Endowment with the spiritual gifts of God.

Other benefits of sacred conversation with God are summarized below:

A). Revelation gifts.

a). ***Word of knowledge***

The gift to operate in the word of Knowledge enables a person to have a clear understanding or deep mental grasp of supernatural issues that would not be possible without God's intervention. This is a gift of God, but can only be received through intimacy with him in prayer.

b). ***Word of wisdom.***

The bible describes two forms of wisdom; the wisdom of the world, and the one that comes from God. Prayer is the major source of divine wisdom. This ability to properly apply knowledge is a gift of God, not given to all, but a reward to deep seeking believers (Proverbs 2:6). Not to the lazy Christian who may find no use of it, or to the fool who does not recognize its source. Wisdom influences actions and helps in taking good decisions.

As a person earnestly prays the revealed word of God, he obtains the gift of a calm, inner ability to confront and subdue spiritual and human challenges. Such people acquire a changed perception of life, and find they are better able to handle issues because they have the benefit of divine clarity.

Those with a good attitude of prayer are more likely to exercise sound judgment, than those without it. This is because they possess a great insight in most cases, which is evidence of privileged knowledge from God.

Wise people show a better understanding of people, things, their environment, and society at large, and they are quicker in applying their unusual ability to arrive at prudent decisions, and just conclusions.

King Solomon, the person generally acknowledged as the wisest person that ever lived, gave these insights about divine wisdom:

> ***"Wisdom is good with an inheritance: and by it there is profit to them that see the sun. For wisdom is a defense, and money is a defense: but the excellency of knowledge is, that wisdom giveth life to them that have it". (Ecclesiastes 7: 11-12).***

> ***"Wisdom is better than weapons of war: but one sinner destroyeth much good". (Ecclesiastes 9: 16).***

The wisdom of God brings a person before kings and great men.

Jesus was full of Holy Ghost and wisdom, and all true followers are encouraged to grow and flow in this gift, just like Jesus did.

c). **<u>*Discernment of spirits*</u>**

We live in very dangerous times, in an age of the love of magic, public practice of witchcraft, and the occult. No wonder the bible warned Christians ahead of time to search all spirits whether they be of God.

> ***"Beloved, believe not every spirit, but try the spirits whether they are of God: because many false prophets are gone out into the world" (1John 4:1)***

The gift of discernment of spirits empowers the Christian to see into the spirit realm, determine the source of events, and weigh whether an action is good or bad. This is because the heart of man has become very wicked in his ways, linking most of his actions to the dark world.

B). Power gifts.

Also known as manifestation gifts, these include:

a). __Faith__

There are various identifiable levels of faith that characterize human approach to God in Prayer. These include:

i). No faith (Deuteronomy 32:20; Mark 4:40).
ii). Weak faith (Romans 4:19)
iii). Little faith (Luke 12:28).
iv). Strong faith (Romans 4:20).
v). Great faith (Matthew 15:28).

However, none of the levels listed above can be described as a gift from God. The only manifestations of the concept of faith that can be classified as God's gifts are:

vi). Believing faith or measure of faith (Romans 12:3)

God endows every person with this measure of faith even if they never asked for it. However, it is the stirring of this dormant measure of faith by another person, a circumstance in life, or by the Holy Spirit that awakens the urge for fellowship with God in a life that never felt so before. This also is proof that God sometimes initiates prayer.

vii). Fruit of faith (Galatians 5:22).

The fruit of faith is the spontaneous work of the Holy Spirit upon the praying Christian which can be further developed as the person continues to hear, study, meditate, and grow in the word of God and in fellowship with him (Romans 10:17). This explains why people who are prayerful excel in the virtues of love, joy, and peace. They are more patient, are very gentle, operate generally by God's standard of goodness and faith, all of which are character traits of Christ

viii). Gift of faith

This is the level of faith that gives substance to a believer's hope or expectation. It is a special gift that cannot be manipulated, developed, or controlled. No carnal person qualifies to operate at this level, yet the Holy Spirit bestows it upon Christians by the grace of God.

Among the eight levels of faith mentioned above, only the believing faith, fruit of faith and gift of faith can be classified as divine heritage.

As these measures of gifts are relentlessly exploited standing on the authority of God's word, those who pray applying them, are better poised to take on and overcome greater challenges, than others who do not. This is because they have the brighter hope for a more comfortable resolution of the situation in question than if they acted on their own abilities. When these classes of believers engage God in prayer, they operate above human perception as their focus is more in the spirit realm. They are no more controlled by what they see, feel, hear, or touch, but by what obtains in the plane of the supernatural.

They see reality in the impracticable, and their actions of faith cause the impossible to become possible in the invisible realm, where all things begin.

*b). **Healing***

The gift to heal others and remained healed comes from a believer's constant interaction with God through his word. God's word is the spiritual nutrient that keeps the human spirit and soul in good shape.

> ***"Beloved, I wish above all things that thou mayest prosper and be in health, even as thy soul prospereth" (3 John 1:2).***

As long as the spirit and soul are spiritually healthy, the body in which they reside will remain equally sound.

*c). **Working of miracles***

This is the gift that enables a believer to achieve the suspension of natural law(s) in order to accomplish some supernatural event(s). It takes the working of miracles sometimes to confirm the word of God in the life or mouth of a believer. Yet, no miracle can occur without the vehicle of prayer.

C). Communication gifts

*a). **Gift of prophecy***

This gift confers a one time or repeated privilege of hearing from God, and being able to pass his message across to a person, group, or congregation. It is a gift from God which he bestows upon whomever he chooses.

> ***"For the prophecy came not in old time by the will of man: but holy men of God spake as they were moved by the Holy Ghost" (2 Peter 1:21).***

This ability to be used of the Holy Spirit must not be confused with the gift of the consecrated office of the Prophet.

b). ***Gift of tongues***

By this gift, a Christian's tongue becomes the Holy Spirit's vessel for the purpose of edifying the body of Christ when there is an interpreter present. It can also be given as a gift for private prayer language when a Christian does not know what or how to pray.

c). ***Interpretation of tongues***

This is the ability given by God to the church community to enable the interpretation of any sacred message received and delivered under the anointing of the Holy Spirit.

All these are gifts through which The father, The Son, and The Holy Spirit manifest to mankind, particularly to the body of Christ.

One distinguishing trait of a relentless prayer warrior is the gift to stir the power of God in any human foundation. God bestows special virtues upon his prayerful children in addition to divine foundational endowments given at birth.

It is by regular interaction with God that the spiritually conscious mind can get all these gifts activated and put to use to the glory of God.

PRAYER POINTS.

1). I arrest all the princes of the air interfering with my prayers, in Jesus name.
2). I bind and cast into dry places, all powers of darkness delaying my answered petitions, in Jesus name.
3). I recover all my stolen blessings from satanic robbers, in Jesus name.
4). O Lord arise, and defend your interest in my life, in Jesus name.
5). Thou Lion of Judah, silence the evil lion roaring against my destiny, in Jesus name.
6). Altar of impossibility ministering to my destiny, collapse, in Jesus name.
7). I decree orderliness into every confused situation in my life, in Jesus name.
8). Holy Spirit, inspire me to subdue my problems instead of yielding to them, in Jesus name.
9). Refreshing river of God, flow into my life, in Jesus name.
10). The Lord is my shepherd, I shall not want, in Jesus name.

Conclusion

If you covet anything in this life, let it be to have the knowledge of the basic principles prayer. Let the hunger to pray and be in fellowship with God be an unquenchable desire in your life. Make your heart an altar where the Holy Ghost fire can burn always, a place through which the light of God will ceaselessly glow. Let your mind be focused always on the word of God, while you meditate on it daily without fail. If your body must remain the temple of God, then your heart must symbolically have room for five specific sacred pieces of furniture as was the case in the inner court of the Old Testament tabernacle. These are:

1). The brazen altar of sacrifice. A Christian's life must represent the living sacrifice on the altar of prayer every day.

2). The table of shew-bread, upon which were daily laid twelve fresh loaves of un-leavened bread, indicating the daily nourishing power of the undefiled word your body would require if you must be in tune with God. (1 Corinthians 11:17-32).

3).The golden altar of incense from where goes forth the sweet smelling, smoke representing the daily rising prayer of the saints (1 kings 7:48-50; Revelations 5:8).

4).The seven branched, golden lampstand which symbolize the ever present Spirit of God, the eternal light of his presence that reveals the way through his word as we pray (John 14:6).

5). The ark of covenant. On this ark was the mercy seat. The seat of his presence where his glory sat whenever Moses prayed. This glory is still available and will overshadow that undefiled Christian that will pray in spirit and in truth.

Prayer is the highest of all noble goals, a great virtue for all true believers to possess. That is why it pleases God immensely when a righteous person knocks on the doors of heaven.

When a prayer warrior is on his knees, the whole of the third heaven is placed on the alert causing the city the principalities and evil powers in the kingdom of darkness and the second heavens to be in disarray. A prayerful Christian is God's light to disperse the darkness in this wicked world. The darker the scene, the brighter the Christian's light should glow.

If you are searching for forgiveness of sins, and for mercy, pray.

For unmerited grace, and the compassionate love of God, pray.

For divine peace, and all round prosperity, pray.

For hope, encouragement, undeserved favor, and the blessings of God that make one rich without any sorrow or un-necessary struggles, pray.

If you have enlisted as a soldier in the army of the Lord, you must develop the attitude of prayer, and form the habit of praying in and out of season.

Prayer is the one thing no one can ever do more than enough. While a person can under-pray, no one can ever over pray. A practical prayer life will elevate a person's spiritual status, as well as make backsliding in such a life difficult.

Prayer is the Christian's surest and most reliable divine insurance. So, we all ought to ***"Pray without ceasing"*** (1 Thessalonians 5:17).

PRAYER POINTS.

1). Not my will O Lord, but yours be done in my prayer life, in Jesus name.

2). Curse of hardship standing against me, break, in Jesus name.

3). Blood of Jesus, erase my name from the record of afflictions, in Jesus name.

4). I break every ancestral covenant with poverty, operating in my life, in Jesus name.

5). I command the evil agreement keeping any blood soul-tie in place in my life to be annulled now, in Jesus name.

6). I renounce every consensual oath administered upon my head, in Jesus name.

7). Blood of Jesus, speak for me where-ever any evil sacrifice is speaking against me, in Jesus name.

8). My father, give me a testimony that will inspire prayer in others, in Jesus name.

9). Finger of God, plug me into the socket of divine prosperity, in Jesus name.

10). The grace of God shall disgrace problems in my life, in Jesus name.